Soundings: A Democratic, Student-Centered Education

SOUNDINGS
A Democratic, Student-Centered Education

by
Mark Springer

National Middle School Association
Westerville, Ohio

No success would have been possible, however, had it not been for the support of the Soundings parents who recognized the values in the rhetoric and who believed in the potential of the reality. Their courage and commitment to step outside the mainstream and to allow their children to participate, particularly in this era of traditional re-entrenchment, have been remarkable and inspiring.

Yet our greatest inspiration—and the most significant source of success—comes from the nearly 300 young adolescents who have participated thus far in Soundings. Their desire to learn, their curiosity, their creativity, their enthusiasm, and their joyous spirit bespeak loudly and clearly the message and the impact of empowerment. They are truly the reality beyond the rhetoric.

Mark Springer
September 2006

About the Author

In his 32 years at Radnor Middle School in Wayne, Pennsylvania, Mark Springer has developed and taught interdisciplinary humanities, creative writing, and American Studies programs. He co-directed the school's gifted program for six years before creating, along with co-teacher Ed Silcox, the award-winning Watershed program, which he taught for 12 years. In 1998, Mark launched the Soundings program described here as an integrative and democratic alternative curriculum for eighth grade students. He also encouraged two of his fellow teachers to develop a comparable program for sixth graders, Crossroads, that is now operating.

Mark is recognized nationally as an exemplary classroom teacher and a strong advocate for the middle school concept. The author of many articles on integrative studies and two books about Watershed, Mr. Springer frequently presents workshops for school districts, civic organizations, professional conferences, and middle level teacher institutes. He also took the photographs used in this book. Mark has served on policy committees for National Middle School Association and in various advisory roles for several publishers. In addition to other honors, Mr. Springer received National Middle School Association's 2004 Distinguished Educator Award.

CONTENTS

Foreword

Keeping the Great Tradition

James A. Beane

There is a long and very special tradition in the education field whereby great teachers write about the programs and approaches they create. Several examples come to mind: Meredith Smith writing before 1920 about her community studies with young children in Pittsburgh that would set the stage for curriculum integration, Francis Sweeney and her colleagues in New York in the 1920s describing their junior high school interdisciplinary units, Gertude Noar explaining the problem-centered core classes in Philadelphia junior high schools in the 1940s, and Rosalind Zapf in the 1950s describing the democratic processes in her high school classroom in Detroit. Mark Springer's *Soundings* is in that great tradition and an excellent addition to it.

Soundings both elevates and educates us. Like his predecessors in the tradition, Mark works with us on two levels. One is as a theorist, explaining with remarkable clarity the "why" beyond the extraordinary programs he and his teaching partners have created. This is not just a program or an approach or a method, it is a philosophy—about the purpose of schools, about teaching and learning, and about our obligations to young people. Many people seem to think that theory and philosophy are for professors while teachers are simply "practitioners." Guess again! Mark Springer, teacher, is a fine theorist. And he has the skill to let us in on the theories with his own words and those of his students.

The other level at which *Soundings* serves us well is the practical. Here we get a deep look into how such a program is created and how it actually works. We are let in on details like how to build community, plan with students, pull together significant and engaging activities, and create assessments worth doing. For good reason, educators almost always respond to new ideas with "give me an example." Well, here it is, both thorough and thoughtful.

Many readers will want to immediately create their own Soundings programs. Be careful. As Mark tells us, this was a program that evolved over time and with a great deal of thought and planning. Moreover, this is his and his teaching partners' program. What is important for us is not that we recreate Soundings, but that we think seriously about doing something like it. How can I turn my classroom into a more democratic space? How can I build community in my classroom? How can I involve students in planning our work together? How can I reach out to find great resources and imaginative activities? How can I work with students to create thoughtful and authentic assessments?

Some places have conditions that might restrict the answers to those questions. Other places do not. The point is that we should all be asking these questions and trying to find whatever answers we can. And there may be as many different answers as there are classrooms and schools. In the end, that is a good thing. We don't need schools where everyone tells the same story. What we need are many stories telling how we might move ahead under varying conditions and by various paths. This is, after all, the great tradition of teachers writing about their work.

We are living in a time when so much of the news about education is depressing and discouraging. Here is fresh air of the best kind. Amidst the intense life of a classroom teacher, it could not have been easy to find the time to write this book. No doubt telling the story will bring some criticism from those who balk at the kinds of approaches and commitments involved in Soundings, so there had to be some courage involved too. I am grateful to Mark Springer for making his work public and for keeping that great tradition alive. And if you want the best for young people, if you want democracy brought to life, if you want an example to lead the way—you will be grateful too.

CHAPTER ONE

A Critique of the Reality

*I think that the heart of a democratic classroom is
that it is all about the students.* — David S.

In this simple utterance, David, an eighth grade member of the first Soundings class in 1998, captured the essence not merely of this program, but of learning as well. Education is supposed to be all about the students. In a democracy, we are supposed to be providing our young citizens with the thinking skills, the knowledge, and the attitudes to debate issues and make informed decisions for the welfare of all. This is not intended to be idle rhetoric, but reality.

The issue of what constitutes a proper education and whether schools are providing it receives a great deal of press and a lot of shelf space these days. Lately, educational reform has become the topic of many discourses, discussions, and debates everywhere from faculty lounges, to corporate boardrooms, to political back rooms. Indeed, we have an entire federal policy now that claims no child will be left behind: surely that indicates that we are "all about the students."

Yet, when one looks closely at schools, particularly those schools attempting to educate young adolescents, one comes away wondering if we are indeed focusing on the students and what they need to become informed and effective citizens. Fragmented schedules based on separate subject classes; classrooms with too many students; standards that emphasize covering far too much material in each class; scripted lesson plans; standardized tests designed to hold students, teachers, and administrators accountable for promoting memorization of the trivial; and an unduly high value placed on grade acquisition rather than knowledge acquisition—all these attributes of today's educational system call into question our sincerity as we claim to be "all about the students." It seems apparent to me that the message is in the medium, and the medium of schools today loudly screams, "Get the scores up, no matter what!"

The 19th century factory model of education seems once again to be in ascendancy: good old-fashioned reading and writing and 'rithmetic taught to the tune of high-stakes hickory sticks, we are told, will solve what ails this country. Unfortunately, the real underlying message in this approach is that the students don't matter as people, but only as test score statistics. We are losing sight of the very students we are supposed to be "all about." I guess one can claim to have left no child behind if you never saw children to begin with.

Important to a democratic society are higher-level thinking skills of analysis, reflection, self-assessment, and synthesis, along with creativity.

Please don't get me wrong: I'm not arguing that reading, writing, and arithmetic aren't vital parts of educating young citizens—they most certainly are crucial. I am arguing that those skills are not enough in and of themselves to ensure the survival of democracy and the freedoms it entails. As important to a democratic society are higher-level thinking skills of analysis, reflection, self-assessment, and synthesis, along with creativity. Cooperation is more important than obedience in a democracy; community solves more problems than competition.

Furthermore, the "get the scores up, no matter what" mentality so prevalent these days seems bent on ignoring the root causes of many of the problems our young people face. It seems to imply that if we spend all our time preparing for high-stakes tests, we won't have to worry about wellness issues such as substance abuse, violence, hunger, sexual activity, physical abuse, depression, and anxiety. Yet these problems don't disappear simply because we ignore them. In fact, ignorance makes them worse. As these problem issues worsen, real learning decreases and our democracy is weakened. What is more, the situation is aggravated when our educational institutions implement strategies that actually increase unhealthy tensions, apathy, and alienation.

This is by no means a new argument. The debate concerning whether to worry about test scores or worry about the whole child has been going on at least since the early 1900s, and probably much longer. The debate was integral to the creation of the junior high school early in the first part of the 20th century and to the development of the middle school in the last quarter of that century. Indeed, the entire middle level philosophy, as expressed vividly in *This We Believe* (National Middle School Association, 2003) is predicated on the belief that "for students to be successful, the school's organization, curriculum, pedagogy, and programs must be based upon the developmental readiness, needs, and interests of young adolescents" (p. 1). Middle level proponents have been advocating this idea for years. Sadly, implementation beyond the rhetoric remains the exception rather than the rule. Our schools continue to follow outdated, undemocratic conventions originally designed more to train illiterate immigrants to be efficient and obedient factory workers and soldiers, rather than full-fledged participants in a democratic process. No Child Left Behind, for all its superficial lip service of concern for individuals, is in many ways just a new package for the old elitist, conservative policies that endeavor to keep meaningful education out of the hands of the many by reducing public education to the lowest common denominator.

We see additional evidence of this in the movement to privatize education and to provide vouchers for religious and private schools. Not surprisingly, the same people who promote the "businessification" of schools also publish the standardized tests and the textbooks. The result is a system designed to perpetuate failure for the already disenfranchised and ultimately, I suspect, to eliminate public education altogether. If and when that occurs, democracy will also disappear, replaced by an overt social structure akin to the medieval feudal system that denied education to all but the elite and powerful in order that they could maintain their control over society.

As students spend more time and energy on memorization and bubble-filling, they have less time and energy to learn to think and act as effective citizens in a democratic society.

If I sound overly alarmist, I apologize. However, the truth of the matter is that knowledge really is power. By knowledge, however, I do not mean merely the ability to read, to write, or to count. I mean instead the ability to think and act independently, to manipulate information, to understand, and to articulate one's own thoughts successfully. This requires far more than memorization of facts and filling in bubbles on an answer sheet. As students spend more time and energy on memorization and bubble-filling, they have less time and energy to learn to think and act as effective citizens in a democratic society. We may well create a generation of "Trivial Pursuit" or "Jeopardy" champions who cannot solve real-world problems or make sensible decisions. By so doing, we relinquish not only our power but also our students' control over their own future. In short, we give away the very rights that education is supposed to be protecting and perpetuating. The specter looming over us in the guise of No Child Left Behind is frightening indeed, and no one should doubt its true intentions.

Fortunately, we can exorcise this demon. We have the knowledge; we have the skills; we even have the technology. Do we have the will to look behind the rhetoric and see the horrific reality our present course entails? Do we have the will to take a fresh look at a different, more progressive and democratic rhetoric and explore its possibilities for helping all our students rise above the mundane and mediocre? I think we do have that courage. I think we have to have that courage. And I think David gave us the mantra and the direction.

The heart of a democratic classroom
is that it is all about the students.

CHAPTER TWO

The Vision Takes Shape

*Now I have learned that we have structure, it is just that
the structure is different from the traditional structure that
we had in the past.* — Chris S.

I started my teaching career 30-plus years ago at almost exactly the
same time that National Middle School Association was founded.
I had the great fortune to be hired by one of Pennsylvania's first
middle schools, already five years into its progressive experience. The
school of about 1,100 students was divided into three houses, or schools-
within-a-school, each with an equal share of the sixth, seventh, and
eighth graders placed on interdisciplinary teams. The curriculum boasted
numerous electives, small advisories, a rotating block schedule, team and
individual teacher planning time, an incredible "lunchblock" program of
clubs and activities, and outstanding intramural and interscholastic sports
programs. In short, it had all the trappings of a true middle school as
defined at that time, and we tried diligently to meet the needs of young
adolescents as best we could in light of that current definition.

We learned a lot over the next few years, even as a major drop in
student population down to fewer than 500 students at one point in the
mid-1980s and the consequent loss of staff forced the abandonment
of the house system, the lunchblock program, the advisories, and many
of the electives. Perhaps more than anything, we began to realize that
middle school philosophy was not merely the sum of these more or
less physical attributes or offerings. Declining enrollment forced some
of us to look at curriculum—at the way we teach and the way students

learn—in a much more critical fashion. Being pushed backwards toward the old junior high school schedule structure and being confronted with a resurgence of the reactionary "back-to-basics" movement made some of us rethink what it meant to "be based upon the developmental readiness, needs, and interests of young adolescents."

In 1985, my teaching partner at that time, Ed Silcox, and I were co-directing the school's gifted program. We were using a modified revolving door process that pulled "gifted" students from their regular classes to pursue areas of personal interest for limited amounts of time. Students negotiated a contract with one of us to mentor their research and presentations, and we then negotiated time and conditions with the classroom teachers. Though this process had many drawbacks, not the least of which was the very label of "giftedness," it taught Ed and me a number of valuable lessons. First and foremost, it proved to us how incredibly capable and dedicated young adolescents are when empowered to follow their strongest learning interests. We saw the benefits of getting to work one on one with students, as well as the benefits of using primary and firsthand resources instead of textbooks. We learned about the power of reflection and self-assessment. And we gained a new perspective on the damage being done by even the best and most well-intentioned teachers working within the traditional curriculum.

We came to believe, based on our experiences working with students, that the following conditions are needed to ensure maximum learning.

Essential tenets of middle level education

1. Successful learning is directly tied to the students' senses of self-investment and self-discipline, their commitment, and their willingness to accept responsibility.

2. The characteristics in number one above are most readily achieved when students are permitted the opportunity to practice them within a supportive atmosphere of encouragement teamed with high expectations.

3. Primary learning skills are processes, not sets of facts. These processes, which are used to handle information, are more important than any particular set of facts.

4. Methods involving hands-on and firsthand learning through self-motivated discovery and reliance on primary resource materials are more effective than secondhand methods. Students should talk more, teachers less.

5. Integrated learning methods more closely match natural learning styles because they focus the learner's attention directly onto relationships, higher-level thinking skills, and processes of application.

6. Traditional letter grade systems cannot adequately reflect the emphasis on processes. Furthermore, such grades too often become ends in themselves without concern for the learning that is the true aim of education. Therefore, written comments ought to be used to describe the students' ongoing development and achievements. These comments provide useful information that specifically recognizes the students' accomplishments while delineating areas that need further attention and improvement.

As these tenets became more firmly rooted in our thinking through the successes of our students using the contract system, and as the limitations imposed by that system and its interaction with the inherently restrictive conventional curriculum became ever more apparent, Ed and I began redefining what middle level education ought to be like. Based on our philosophy, we formulated this list of basic characteristics:

Underlying characteristics: The shared vision

1. Students must have vested interest and shared control over their learning.

2. Learning must be process and performance based.

3. Learning must be based on real-world and real-work relevance and firsthand experiences.

4. Learning must be integrative.

5. Learning methods should emphasize cooperation rather than competition.

6. Learning is better facilitated within an atmosphere of respect, concern, and support wherein the learner feels safe and comfortable.

7. The teacher's role is that of mentor and guide.

8. The teachers must model the desired behaviors and attitudes.

9. Parents and the community at large should be integral parts of the learning process.

Ed and I then set out to design a curriculum that would incorporate all these characteristics. By 1985, we had chosen the watershed theme because everything that occurs on planet earth happens in a watershed. Thus, anything a student needs or wants to study could be connected directly to a watershed. At the same time, the concept of watersheds gave us a recognizable academic center from which we could cull knowledge and toward which we could apply skills associated with the traditional curricular disciplines. The watershed theme seemed at the time to represent the perfect confluence of student empowerment and institutional imperatives. So, from the tenets and characteristics listed above, the Watershed Program, with these objectives, took shape.

Objectives of the Watershed Program

1. To create a learning environment in which the students accept responsibility for their learning.

2. To provide students with an awareness of the relevance of learning and of their personal connections with the materials covered, and to demonstrate the interrelatedness of all learning.

3. To emphasize the importance of fundamental thinking and communication skills, and to encourage learning from primary rather than secondary (e.g., textbook) sources.

4. To create a learning environment that promotes cooperative rather than competitive learning.

5. To illustrate that education is best achieved when it is a cooperative venture shared by teachers, students, and parents; and, to that end, to maximize parental involvement in the learning process.

6. To demonstrate that effective learning is a lifelong pursuit that transcends the limits of the school's walls.

7. To emphasize the ecological, historical, economic, political, and cultural importance of watersheds.

In 1987, we launched the Watershed Program as an experiment in integrated curriculum—an attempt to build a cohesive curriculum that was truly "all about the students."

The program proved remarkably successful from the start and continues to provide seventh graders at our school with an amazing, student-centered, integrated experience. What is more, over the last two decades, countless visitors from around the world have spent time in the Watershed classroom and have taken home with them all or at least parts of the program to institute in their schools.

Now in its 20th year, Watershed continues to provide a meaningful education for seventh graders.

Despite the success of Watershed, by the time James Beane published *A Middle School Curriculum: From Rhetoric to Reality* in 1993, I was already beginning to feel the need to push the envelope even further. Reading Jim's book, I began to realize that while Watershed empowered our students to an unprecedented extent, it didn't go far enough. Watershed met all eight of Jim's "guidelines for a middle school curriculum" (pp. 17-23), at least on the surface; but too many decisions continued to be made by Ed and me. The curriculum was becoming too predictable, too much the same from year to year, maybe even too conventional.

The publication of *Watershed: A Successful Voyage into Integrative Curriculum* (Springer, 1994) gave me new access and new perspectives. I got to know Jim Beane and Barb Brodhagen, as well as a number of other practitioners of integrative curricula such as Wally Alexander, Kathy McAvoy, Dennis Carr, and Gert Nesin. I gained opportunities to discuss middle level philosophy and curriculum integration with pioneers of the middle school movement. Experts such as Gordon Vars, Chris Stevenson, Ed Brazee, Nancy Doda, John Lounsbury, and Sue Thompson, among others—all forceful and articulate advocates for the empowerment of young adolescents—gave me ideas and inspiration. These discussions further clarified my thoughts and cemented my resolve to move beyond Watershed to an even more fully integrative program for middle level learners—to make the growing rhetoric a heightened reality.

Conditions at my school, however, were not yet right. For one thing, the principal at that time, while supportive, was not prepared to expand the integrated program. He was openly reluctant to allow other teachers to experiment with teaming or teaching approaches similar to

Watershed. The school now faced overcrowding, so room for another integrated program was also an issue.

The following school year, 1995–96, saw a new opportunity open up to initiate a more fully integrative curriculum. An outside audit team from Lehigh University presented its report (White, 1996) on the state of our middle school. That report asserted that one of our school's strengths was Watershed. The report stated: "The Watershed Project is recognized by staff, community and parents as an excellent and challenging integrated program. It can serve as a workable model for other subject areas and grade levels for increasing interdisciplinary learning at Radnor Middle School" (p. 1). The panel then concluded: "In addition, we strongly recommend that an interdisciplinary program be developed at eighth grade as an extension of the Watershed Program" (p. 24). This outside endorsement, while not welcomed by the traditionalists on staff, certainly provided impetus to our administration to consider another alternative program. The principal asked me to convene a committee to study integrated alternatives for our sixth and eighth grades.

This committee met many times during the subsequent year and a half, but all of our proposals met subtle yet firm resistance from the building administration. Then, in the spring of 1997, the principal resigned; and our longtime assistant principal, himself a strong supporter of Watershed, became our principal. Within a few months, our committee had a proposal ready for the district's curriculum committee to consider.

Hence, in September of 1998, 40 eighth graders, my new teaching partner, Sheila LaBriola, and I began constructing the first Soundings Program. That first exciting, frightening, and truly exhilarating year exceeded expectations and shot to the top of my list of favorite experiences. Despite unfortunate circumstances affecting staffing and room locations that have buffeted and threatened the program since

As a successful, outside-the-box program, Soundings attracts visitors from near and far.

its inception, Soundings has slowly established itself as an academic force. Despite the current political climate that promotes a philosophy of education diametrically opposed to that of Soundings, the program grows in its reputation for excellence, for high expectations for all its students, and for the democratic empowerment of young adolescents. More and more visitors come each year, and I am called upon more and more often to share the program through articles and presentations.

Yet I remain frustrated by the slow pace of change in education, a pace further slowed by the hostile political forces that would try to reverse our progress toward student-centered curricula and drag us back to 19th century curricular models in the guise of 21st century progress. I remain frustrated as well by the number of people who hear or read overviews and summaries of the program but can't quite grasp the reality of the rhetoric. Visitors who spend several days or a week in the Soundings classroom leave with a clearer vision of its power, but few have so much time to spend with us. Most visitors come for only a day or for just a few hours. They get only a brief glimpse into the world of curriculum integration, the amazing benefits it holds for young adolescents, and the advantages it has over conventional curricular practices. Yet, from even these short visits, they leave us in awe of the students and their abilities and accomplishments.

So I sought a way to get the message across more clearly and more completely. Many have suggested to me that it would be helpful if I went through the curriculum integration process step by step, just as it unfolds in the Soundings classroom over an entire year, and used specific examples of the questions, themes, projects, and processes developed in cooperation with the students. They want me to show them in detail the different structure of curriculum integration and how it is truly all about the students.

This volume seeks to fulfill the request for a detailed, yearlong account, one that will provide the reality that proves the rhetoric.

CHAPTER THREE

The Rhetoric Reaffirmed

*The students have just as much input on things as the teachers
do. That makes me feel like I'm somebody, and that we are smart
enough to handle the responsibility.* — Mollie J.

Before starting our in-depth examination of curriculum integration
as it plays out in the Soundings Program, it would be helpful to
establish some working vocabulary. It is crucial for all of us to
understand what we mean by this term *curriculum integration*. It has been
used widely in the past 10 or 15 years and often has not been applied as
accurately or as appropriately as it ought to be. I've heard many different
definitions of curriculum integration and integrative curricula, and they
usually differ from the meaning I intend to use here.

I want to be very clear that I am not using it to indicate the simple
blending of content and skills around a central theme. Though that is
an obvious and important component, it is not the heart and soul of the
process. I have myself often used a curriculum continuum (Brazee &
Capelluti, 1995, pp. 28-29) to illustrate how an integrative curriculum
approaches content relative to the conventional curriculum with which
most educators are familiar. However, to stop at that illustration is to
miss the larger and more significant issues that focus on the student
rather than subject area connections. The outward manifestation may
be a theme-based approach "without regard for subject area boundaries"
(Beane, 1997, p. xi), but the processes involved focus on integrating
personal and social experiences and knowledge to affect the equitable
democratic empowerment of students. As another of my students,
Christine, said, "In addition to this, [we] are also learning the way a

democratic society works, as well as how to cooperate with all types of people. I think this is a great way of learning."

While I will leave more detailed philosophical and historical explanations to James Beane, who is far more articulate than I, suffice it here to say that curriculum integration goes far beyond the conventional strategies, which are concerned mainly with acquisition of information. It is designed to help students "integrate curriculum experiences into their schemes of meaning and to experience the democratic process of problem solving" relative to issues "of personal and social significance in the real world" (Beane, 1997, p. 9).

By so doing, I contend, curriculum integration takes as its ultimate aim helping students learn to live better lives now as well as in the future, not merely gathering more information for possible use later. As yet another of my students, Jordan, put it, "A characteristic of Soundings is that we are given opportunities to experiment with a different learning method, the firsthand learning experience, which supplies us with not only knowledge for school, but knowledge for life." This not-so-subtle shift from an emphasis on subject matter to a focus on the student allows us to construct a curriculum designed to address a wide range of student needs.

Curriculum integration takes as its ultimate aim helping students learn to live better lives now as well as in the future, not merely gathering more information for possible use later.

This is particularly crucial at the middle level as young adolescents are striving to achieve a sense of personal identity at the same time that they are confronting the world at large to a more significant extent than most have during their elementary years. Throw into this mix major physical changes and the psychological, emotional, and intellectual repercussions of that physical growth and maturity, and it is clear that young adolescents face a difficult time during which "achieving academic success is highly dependent upon their other developmental needs being met" (NMSA, 2003, p. 3).

While we as a society have long recognized how turbulent adolescence is, we have tended to downplay it when it comes to taking action. It is as if we take adolescence for granted as little more than a nasty inconvenience, a stage to be endured with clenched teeth, but one that will ultimately pass. We seem to have selective memory, somehow blocking out what was too painful to remember and focusing instead on the fact that we survived. This apparently allows us to believe further that each subsequent generation of young adolescents will do the same, and thus we need not actually do anything to help them.

Am I overly cynical? Perhaps, but it seems to me that justification for my cynicism is obvious and irrefutable. One needs look no further than Columbine or Red Lake or a dozen other incidents of shootings in schools in recent years. Even a cursory look at statistics on eating disorders, bullying, teen suicide, depression, substance abuse, crime, or dropouts reveals that many of our young adolescents do not, in fact, survive this "stage" at all, let alone pass through it unscathed.

At the same time, look at our schools. What changes have we seen in response to the alarming statistics? Despite the lip service paid to the problems of young adolescents in contemporary culture, and despite some superficial changes in the direction of middle level philosophy, nothing substantive has changed on a systemic level. Schools remain much as they have been for the last century or so.

Some more reactionary elements have tried to blame the situation on middle level philosophy itself. These forces, often with hidden political agendas, call for a return to harsh, strict, punitive measures reminiscent of the Puritan era. However, as many other leaders have been quick to point out, in many ways that is precisely what schools have always been. Progressive educational practices, such as curriculum integration, have never become anywhere near the norm. Most schools called "middle schools" still maintain much of the old junior high school when it comes to curricular substance. Yet, where integrative practices exist in full measure, they have proven remarkably more successful in helping young adolescents through these turbulent years while simultaneously educating those same students well academically (Dickinson, 2001; Kohn, 1999, 2004; Jackson & Davis, 2000; Springer, 1994).

Where integrative practices exist in full measure, they have proven remarkably more successful in helping young adolescents through these turbulent years while simultaneously educating those same students well academically.

In particular, Soundings and similar integrative curricula focus on the needs of young adolescents to establish a sense of self, to belong to a group that provides safety and support, and involve them in meaningful learning activities with tangible results. Studies abound that have identified the essential needs of young adolescents. Here are just four such lists from different sources.

1. Identity—to be recognized as a part of something unique, special

2. Bonding—to be included in something meaningful, something with a sense of family

3. Competence—to feel successful at something—if necessary, even in areas not valued by society

4. Safety—to feel mentally and physically secure

5. Change—to be a part of something different and exciting

6. Meaning—to be part of something that accepts them while offering a reason for being

Adapted from: Gonzales, Luis (1991). *Why Youth Gang Up. Gang Free Zones.* Center for Gang Free Schools and Communities. Cited in: Lounsbury, John (1996). Please, Not Another Program. *ClearingHouse, 69* (4).

1. Security

2. Self-Image and Self-Esteem

3. Affiliation

4. Motivation/Mission

5. Achievement/Competence

Adapted from: Borba, Dr. Michele (1996). *Esteem Builders Complete Program.* Austin, TX: Jalmar Press.

1. Climate of acceptance, tolerance, emotional safety, guidance

2. Choice, responsibility, accountability, appropriate challenge, relative success

3. Opportunities to develop range of skills and pursue variety of content areas

4. Complex subject matter, relevant issues

5. Higher-level analytical questioning, time and opportunity for critical thinking

6. Self-evaluation

7. Opportunity to interact with knowledgeable adults in collaborative projects

8. Emphasis on cooperation, inclusiveness, group contribution

9. Structured, positive student interaction

Adapted from: Beamon, Glenda Ward (2001). *Teaching With Adolescent Learning in Mind.* Arlington Heights, VA: Skylight Professional Development.

1. A sense of relatedness, of belonging

2. A sense of self-determination, the ability to make decisions about things that affect us

3. Opportunities to feel effective

4. Opportunities to learn new things that matter to us and to answer personally meaningful questions

Adapted from: Kohn, Alfie (2004). *Constant Frustration and Occasional Violence. What Does It Mean to Be Well Educated?* Boston: Beacon Press.

The first thing one notes is how similar the lists are. The terminology may differ slightly, but the meaning is consistent. I think most adults who actually work with young adolescents would readily concur that these lists accurately capture the essential needs of our students.

Now spend just a few minutes in typical middle level and high schools. Here one immediately experiences a world that does not address these needs (Sizer 1984, 1992). In fact, as I have argued for years, the conventional system by its very structure often works in blatant opposition to these needs. All we need do is list even a few of the realities we see in most schools, and the contrast becomes apparent.

The conventional curricula and organization work against student needs in these ways:

- Scheduling practices and tracking isolate and even alienate students.

- A sense of group identity is difficult to achieve as students shift from one group to another throughout the day.

- Students don't have adequate opportunity to get to know adults well.

- Schedules of 45-minute chunks preclude extended exploration and reflective thinking.

- Curricula are created around isolated subject areas that kids study without transition or interconnection.

- Content is presented without establishing its relevance for students' lives.

- Grades rather than learning are emphasized.

Is it any wonder why kids see school as irrelevant or boring and why cheating is accepted? The lack of shared group identity and the lack of any sense of ownership or connection to the content foster many negative side effects. According to a national survey, 30% of students in grades six to ten are involved in moderate or frequent bullying as victims, bullies, or both (Nansel et al., 2001). And let's remember that bullying is not limited to physical abuse: social and psychological abuses are equally devastating. Think about the ways some of our conventional school practices can lead to social and psychological damage—grading, class rankings, fear, embarrassment, and intimidation used by teachers to maintain control. We employ high-stakes standardized tests that evoke fear and increase pressure on students—and teachers alike—tests that often focus on the trivial rather than the universal, and on memorization, not thought. We emphasize competition, winning at another's expense, and power acquisition; and then we wonder why students bully each other.

These examples represent just the tip of the iceberg. Spend any time at all in many schools, and the list of ways we work against rather than for the students grows longer. At the teacher level, I certainly know this is not intentional. I have never met a teacher who went into the profession because he or she wanted to hurt young people. Many, however, don't seem to have given much serious thought to why they teach as they do. They went through school and were taught this way. Then they took teacher-training courses that reinforced traditional pedagogy and conventional curricula. Once in the field, some begin to sense something is not quite right; but very few, if any, have experience with alternatives, and most see the bureaucracy as a daunting obstacle to change.

Nevertheless, we must change. Staying the same is falling behind in a world that moves forward with increasing speed. It is time to realize that we cannot maintain the status quo and expect young adolescents to be prepared to function successfully in a democratic society that will expect them to manipulate information, not store it.

Curriculum integration espouses a number of ideas that can have a positive impact on our students and move us closer to a system that fulfills their needs. For example, curriculum integration calls for smaller learning communities with more time together to build healthy, supportive relationships. It advocates using democratic classrooms and student empowerment, along with theme-based curricula developed from student-generated questions. Curriculum integration places emphasis on quality over mere quantity and understanding over memorization, and on authentic assessment including student self-assessment. And there are other benefits.

Furthermore, I agree with Tom Dickinson (2001) who writes in *Reinventing the Middle School* that this middle level "concept is a totally integrated ecology of schooling" (p. 4), the likes of which few of us have ever seen before, and that implementing a limited number of the complex pieces involved weakens the potential of the system. Curriculum integration cannot be done piecemeal—a point we will return to later.

So, in light of current conditions and known needs, a comprehensive and systemic change is required. We need to build small, democratic learning communities that can provide a safe environment and a sense of belonging. We need to use students' questions as the basis for themes to study. We need to create with our students activities that will have both personal meaning and larger significance in the real world.

A tall order to be sure, but not an impossible task. So let's put the rhetoric aside for awhile—but by no means forget it—and examine the reality of Soundings. Let's immerse ourselves in this example of curriculum integration. Let's probe the depths of its methods to see one way a true community of learners has been established and maintained through curriculum integration. Be aware, however, that this description is not intended to be a prescription. As Jim Beane (2005) wisely points out in *A Reason to Teach*, "Teaching the democratic way cannot be lifted from another school or classroom" (p. 121) because it is a community process tied directly to the particular individuals collectively working within it. The examples in the following chapters are not lesson plans to be used like a textbook or teacher-proof curriculum from a publishing company. Every year is different, just as every group of students is different. Yes, they ask similar questions and select similar themes, but each is ultimately a fresh and unique exploration into student-centered issues. That is why I try in what follows to present some of the multiplicity of techniques and strategies we have used in Soundings. The reader should take from these examples their essence, and then apply that to his or her own circumstances and substance.

The true reality of curriculum integration and democratic learning exists when students purposefully experience democracy in the classroom. All the rest is rhetoric.

CHAPTER FOUR

Moving Into Action:
Building a Community of Learners

*Everyone in the group has to learn how to accept other people's
ideas and not only use his or her own. We have to learn how to work
together and cooperate with each other.*   — Ashley L.

In order to establish and maintain a democratic community of learners
in which the needs of young adolescents can be met, a structure must
be created that promotes discussion among all the members. Thus it
is necessary to keep the community small, keep it in one place, and allow
it sufficient, uninterrupted time.

I am certainly not unique or alone in the realization that smaller is
better when it comes to education. The National Forum to Accelerate
Middle-Grades Reform, for example, released a policy statement in
2004 asserting that "smallness . . . is a necessary but not sufficient
organizational structure that enhances teaching and learning at the
middle level" (p. 1). The policy paper goes on to describe in some detail
the advantages of small learning communities and backs up the claims
with research documentation. George and Lounsbury (2000), when
supporting smallness, noted:

> The public school is the one major institution in the best
> position to counter the trend toward impersonal, bureaucratic
> operations. As typically organized, however, middle and high
> schools are a part of the problem rather than a part of the

21

solution. Implementing one of the ways to provide a sense of smallness can put schools in the solution category. (p. 113)

I could go on and cite a growing body of research in support of creating smaller learning communities. We need to recognize, however, that maximum advantage is attained only when other optimum conditions are met, including those of time, space, and pedagogy, as well as size. Any compromises deemed necessary for a particular school's situation will result in some reduction in the overall effectiveness of the process. Practitioners and prospective practitioners must weigh carefully the compromises proposed with an eye to the limiting impact those concessions may entail.

For example, in Soundings, we limit our population to 40 students and two teachers who share one large room. This number was determined by our administration to retain parity with the traditional class sizes in our school. In an ideal world, the learning community would be even smaller, 24–30. In fact, I once proposed that our school adopt a partner-team approach for the entire population. Two teachers would share a room with a set number of students all day, and all subject areas would be thematically integrated, as is the case in our three existing integrated programs. The resulting team sizes would be about 24 students; and that would be with no change up or down in present staffing levels.

The early use of table groups is vital in building community.

However, acceptance of such a radical change requires time, so we have found 40 students is a very workable, if not ideal, number. Nevertheless, we recognize that the number lengthens the time required for full discussions. I have heard of groups trying to use this process with up to 60 students, but I would question the efficacy of so large a group. First of all, this usually necessitates using separate rooms for all or most of the time. As soon as you split the group, you impede the formation of community.

Similarly, the significantly larger number of voices clearly slows the process and calls for additional strategies to ensure that all are heard.

Providing our time together

The process of building community does take time. Democracy is a messy business. Each student's voice needs to be heard and each idea validated. Hence, the more time one can allot to curriculum integration the better. I would prefer to have my students all day, every day; but Soundings works on a schedule centered around a three-hour block of time representing periods 3, 4, 5, and 7, broken only for a half-hour lunch period. When students choose to eat in the Soundings room, as they regularly do, this gives them what amounts to three and a half hours of solid community work time.

In addition, we enjoy several smaller meeting sessions during the day. These shorter time periods include the school's 22-minute advisory period first thing in the morning, which we generally use to address many of the housekeeping details—announcements, handing out various forms, filling out self-assessments, collecting homework, and the like. We also have the closing 40 minutes of the day, a period our school dubs Community Resource Time, CRT for short, during which band, orchestra, chorus, and student council meet on different days. Students involved in these are not in Soundings on the days assigned to these activities, but others are in our room. They use this time to work on their individual responsibilities and get additional one-on-one help.

A group seeks help in determining its direction from my co-teacher, Sheila.

Finally, we also use one of the students' four elected specials time slots to meet with smaller groups in what we call Soundings Workshop. During the first semester one half of the class is split into two groups, and each group has this additional period on an alternating day basis. The other half of the community does the same in the second semester. Again, this allows us to work very closely with individual students without taking away from the larger community's block of time.

For roughly one third of their day, Soundings students are reintegrated with students from the two large conventional teams. When not in

Soundings, students attend one of several math classes, ranging from remedial to geometry, during first period every day immediately following the advisory time. Similarly, our students daily take a world language of their choice, be it French, Spanish, German, or Latin.

In addition to the math and foreign language classes, Soundings students take required health and physical education classes. They also have one other elective, such as art, music, technology education, or family and consumer science. These classes, like our Soundings Workshop, meet during our second and eighth periods of the day. The school employs a six-day rotation schedule, so elective classes meet every other day for half the year.

Early steps with students and parents to build community

Once these basic logistics have been determined, establishing a shared vision can begin in earnest. For our students this process starts in the spring before their Soundings year. As seventh graders, they hear about the program through a series of orientation presentations and then decide if they would like to participate. This is an important step on at least two levels. First, it gives students a chance to think about the democratic philosophy of learning that curriculum integration entails and decide whether or not they share that part of the vision. Secondly, it embodies that very philosophy by empowering the students to make the initial decision and thus validates the process from the onset. Appendix 1 (p. 153) includes copies of the orientation and selection documents used in 2006–2007 with Soundings VIII.

All the students who express interest in participating are put into a computer, which then randomly generates a class list and a waiting list of alternates. Separate lists for boys and girls are produced to help ensure the class will have an even number of each. This is the only bias built into the process, and it is there to meet a student need. Over the years, I have noted that as young adolescents enter the realm of sexual awareness, they seldom feel comfortable when they are outnumbered by the opposite sex. So we keep the community as gender balanced as possible to limit stress or discomfort.

Once the initial class list has been generated, we meet again, this time with the students and their parents. Parents then hear essentially the same message their children heard and receive a copy of the Participants' Responsibilities. We answer any questions they may have, and we ask them to take their time and discuss the program before making a final decision to participate. Though we give them a week to make up their minds, many turn in the form that evening. If anyone elects not to become a member of the class, the next student on the waiting list gets an invitation to participate.

Clearly this strategy openly invites the parents to be active partners in their children's education and establishes the expectation of two-way communication that will be critical to the effectiveness of the learning community throughout the coming year. The final decision is declared by student and parent signatures on a form that includes short responses to two questions asking the students why they want to be in Soundings and what they hope to add to the class. These essays are for information only. Though they are not assessed in any way, they provide us with a first glimpse into the students' motivations and, on a practical level, their writing skills.

In an evening meeting, parents and potential students find out more about Soundings.

A third meeting of the new class occurs just before the start of the summer break. This time the students who will be the coming year's Soundings class gather in the Soundings room to receive their "summer packet." This packet contains a number of important items intended to help foster elements of the learning community even before the new school year opens. The packet includes a welcome letter, a list of fundamental responsibilities, and a list of materials each student will need to bring to class. These items serve to remind students of the program's objectives and also to give them information to make them feel comfortable as they begin this new adventure.

The packet also contains several items that help establish some of the more academic expectations and responsibilities. The forms needed for our reading journal are there, for example, along with an activity involving literary terms that helps meet our district's language arts standards, a time line assignment related to the district social studies standards, and a brief reading assignment about estuaries that helps fulfill some science standards. In addition, we include short assignments designed to get the students thinking about setting goals and asking questions—two extremely crucial aspects of the Soundings experience.

To nourish further the newly planted sense of community, we invite the students to contact us during the summer. We provide them with our e-mail addresses and ask each one to send us a postcard during vacation to fill us in on summer activities. These postcards are displayed in the room when the students arrive on the first day of school and help to make the students feel as though they are already a part of the room and community. The postcards also serve as a wonderful, informal focus for students to use as they reacquaint themselves with each other and share their summer experiences during the opening days of school.

Finally, we provide students with letters of advice from previous years' students. This establishes a link between the new group and the larger Soundings community that has preceded them. The peer advice also resonates with students who may still be wary, based on earlier school experiences, of teachers' promises. Appendix 2 (p. 158) includes examples of these letters along with all the other summer packet materals.

We enclose two messages to the parents in the summer packet. The first is a letter inviting parents to establish e-mail contact with us. It is important to initiate this offer, as e-mail is clearly the fastest, easiest, and most efficient method now available for communicating with parents; it sure beats playing telephone tag over several days! Yet it is important to grant parents the option of using or not using e-mail. Some parents may not have a computer or may share an e-mail account with their child—though this is becoming less and less of a problem. Some may simply prefer to talk on the phone or face to face. Whatever the reasoning, by giving parents the choice, we demonstrate a subtle form of empowerment that strengthens respectful relationships and enhances communication. It should be noted as well that parents must be assured that phone calls and personal conferences are always options, even if they have elected to use e-mail most of the time. The bottom line is that we make every effort to show parents that we value their input and will do everything possible to listen to their ideas.

The second and equally significant message to parents asks them directly for some of that input: namely, to let us know what their goals are for their child in the Soundings experience. I tell students that this is their parents' summer homework, which indicates all are participating in the workload. Students seem to enjoy this reference as it puts them on a par with their parents, in a manner of speaking, and shows them that goal setting is an adult activity, not merely an academic exercise for students.

Some parents write very short responses emphasizing their desire that the child enjoy the year and gain new perspectives on learning. Others write detailed pages about their child's idiosyncrasies, perceived strengths, and areas that present difficulties. Regardless of the length or the amount of detail, these parental statements provide valuable insights that can help us tailor the Soundings experience more closely to each child's individual needs.

All of this is explained in detail to the students at the meeting in June. Again, the crucial point of all these efforts is to create a spirit of respectful and empowering communication and establish avenues to ensure that communication occurs. This is the first major step in building a strong community of learners. All have to believe that their voices matter, that they will have access to all the necessary information, and that their ideas and concerns will be honored. As teachers, our every action and every word have to embody this philosophy if the necessary level of trust is to be achieved.

Soundings I at the Maritime Museum.

One final thing we do before sending the students off for the summer is take a class portrait. This has been a tradition in our integrated programs since we launched the Watershed Program in the mid-1980s. Class portraits enlarged to poster size (20"x 30") are framed and displayed in chronological order just below the ceiling around the Soundings classroom. The current group's portrait, however, is displayed on the impact wall directly across from the classroom door, so it is one of the very first things the students—or visitors—see when they enter the room. Subtle touches or details such as this let the students know that they are part of a growing tradition and the focus for this year.

And all of this occurs before their Soundings year officially begins in early September.

Soundings VII, 2005–2006.

When other students arrive at school that first day, they have no idea who will be in their advisory, their several classes, or even who most of their teachers will be. Soundings students already know these things and have completed some common assignments and experiences, and enter a room that displays concrete evidence of their presence and ownership—foundations upon which the learning community can readily be built once school opens.

This key message of student ownership is conveyed in other subtle ways as well. For instance, the doors of the rooms assigned to Soundings and the other two integrated programs, Watershed and Crossroads (the sixth grade program), unlike other doors, are totally unadorned, waiting for the students to decide how they want to label and decorate them—a task that will be addressed in the early days of school as one of the many community-building activities that form the programs' foundation for curriculum integration.

Getting underway in September

When the students arrive in September, a number of things occur that implement the Soundings vision. They enter a fairly large room lined with bookshelves and class portraits. Last year's affirmations are still on the walls, waiting to be replaced by this year's; the Soundings logo looms overhead, painted on the ceiling tiles. On the blackboard are the date, the first log question, and a quotation. There is also a section of the board labeled "Ongoing Responsibilities." There students see a list of the first few tasks they will be asked to complete and the due dates. Included will be several of the tasks from the summer packet. These will be collected and used in class over the next several days.

Tables and chairs are arranged around the room in groups of four or six, a pattern that is readily changed as different activities dictate. On the tables at each seat lies a thin three-ring binder with a student's name printed on a card attached to its cover—each student's logbook.

Opening the logbook, the students find a poem, entitled "Dream Big." This will be used in our very first activity once all the students have arrived and settled into the room. Turning the page, they come to a sheet labeled "Personal Goals." On this page the student is asked to list and sign goals for the year. The next page, labeled "Personal Responsibilities" asks the students to respond in writing to this statement: "In order to accomplish my goals and to help my classmates in Soundings accomplish their goals, I consistently need to fulfill the following responsibilities." After these pages come the daily entry sheets, about 50 of them, each holding four days' worth of entries, and then 20 sheets each designed to hold two weeks' quotations and responses.

The daily entry pages have space for the date, the log question, and its answer; a summary of the student's activities and accomplishments; and goals for the next day. This logbook will be the backbone of our work, even as it serves to meet a district journaling standard. The log questions reflect each day's focus and ultimately become a running record of the program's activities. (Appendix 3, p. 177, contains all the log questions used in Soundings VI.) Similarly, the student's summary of accomplishments becomes a valuable self-assessment tool and record of individual achievements, while the goals help the student stay organized and self-directed.

We also have a class logbook that serves a similar purpose for the learning community as a whole. Two different students are assigned to maintain the class logbook each week. A sample of the form is shown below. Note the spaces to record both visitors and absentees. Visitors can scan this class log and get a quick idea of what the class has been doing all year. Absentees will sign the book when they return as they ascertain what they have missed.

We use the class logbook to start class every day. The person acting as recorder for the day before reads his or her entry aloud. Students can offer amendments and additions to the class record based on their individual log entries. This gives students an opportunity to debrief the previous day, and also to publicly highlight events or individual contributions they think worthy of special recognition. As you can imagine, this process, which usually takes about five minutes, helps bond the community through shared experience and recollection. It also helps reinforce community standards, expectations, and goals.

Soundings Class Log, 2004–2005

Date:_____   Recorder:_____

Log Question: _____

_____

Quotation: [Tuesdays/Thursdays]_____

_____

New Assignments: Date Due:

_____   _____

_____   _____

Summary of the Day: _____

_____

Visitors/From: _____

_____

Absentees: _____

Sign-in-upon return_____

On the inside cover pocket of the students' logbooks, we have placed a number of forms that go along with the school's opening day procedures and a few of our own as well. Insurance forms, emergency contact cards, and other forms the school asks us to distribute are handled this way. We discuss them briefly and remind students to take them home for their parents. We also include a form asking the parents to give blanket field trip permission so that we don't have to send home a separate form every time. A similar form asking for parental permission for their child to be interviewed, photographed, and videotaped also goes out so our many visitors can freely interact with the students throughout the year.

As the students enter that first morning, my partner and I greet each one by name and ask about his or her summer, making reference whenever possible to the card that was returned. Having typed their names many times over the summer as I prepared the various class activity lists and having spent time studying the class portrait, I have a pretty good idea of which name goes with which face. I always miss a few, but the students laugh good-naturedly because they recognize and appreciate that I have made a sincere effort to learn their names ahead of time. Mispronunciations are common too, but this also demonstrates to them that I'm not afraid to make mistakes or to admit my errors and sets a tone of trust that will empower students to take similar risks throughout the year. Finally, I ask each student if he or she has a nickname or preferred form of the "official" name that appears on the office-generated lists.

Once all have arrived and have had a few minutes to check out their postcards and class portrait, said hello to friends they haven't seen all summer, and found a seat and logbook, my partner and I welcome them officially. Often, if the weather is nice, we will go immediately outside and form a circle in the yard. If it is too rainy to go out, we remain inside. Either way, I direct their attention to the poem, "Dream Big," already in their log; and then my teaching partner and I read it aloud, alternating lines or verses. The poem, whose author is apparently unknown, can be found readily on the Internet at a wide variety of sites.

This inspirational poem provides an excellent introduction to the curriculum integration concept that challenges the students to take charge of their learning and empowers them to create their own year. The poem emphasizes the power of thinking and dreaming, attaches it directly to individual interests and motivation, and then calls for action to make dreams (dare I say rhetoric?) reality. It could not be more appropriate to the overall task at hand.

The poem also ties in with the year's first log question, which asks the students: *When you think about the coming year, what big dreams do you have for Soundings?* The year's first quotation picks up on the same theme, Shaw's famous statement from *Back to Methuselah* (1921), Act 1: "You see things; and you say, 'Why?' But I dream things that never were; and I say, 'Why not?'"

Dream Big

If there were ever a time to dare,
to make a difference,
to embark on something worth doing,
it is now.
Not for any grand cause, necessarily—
but for something that tugs at your heart,
something that's your aspiration,
something that's your dream.

You owe it to yourself to make your days here count.
Have fun.
Dig deep.
Stretch.

Dream big.

Know, though, that things worth doing seldom come easy.
There will be good days.
And there will be bad days.
There will be times when you want to turn around,
pack it up, and call it quits.
Those times tell you that you are pushing yourself,
that you are not afraid to learn by trying.

Persist.

Because with an idea,
determination, and the right tools,
you can do great things.
Let your instincts,
your intellect,
and your heart guide you.

Trust.

Believe in the incredible power of the human mind.
Of doing something that makes a difference.
Of working hard.
Of laughing and hoping.
Of lazy afternoons.
Of lasting friends.
Of all the things that will cross your path this year.

The start of something new brings the hope of something great.
Anything is possible.
There is only one you.
And you will pass this way only once.

Do it right.

We will introduce these two elements back in the room; but first, while we're already in a circle, it is a good time to play our first cooperative game. We use a lot of cooperative challenge games throughout the year as an important way to build and maintain community. These challenges encourage teamwork, often involve problem-solving skills, and always provide an enjoyable break from seatwork. I've assembled a repertoire of challenge activities over the years from a variety of sources, including workshops and books such as the *New Games* (Fluegelman, 1976) books that were popular in the 1970s.

For this first challenge, we like to play "Beep" or "Pulse." It is a simple game in which the players hold hands and pass a hypothetical electric current around the circle by gently squeezing the hand of their immediate neighbor while uttering a sound such as "beep." The challenge is to see how quickly the group can get the pulse around the circle.

After explaining the basic objective of the game, I always ask the students to think about what actions will be required if we are to be successful. Obviously, this means everyone has to cooperate and pay attention, and the students are quick to recognize this. We then try to guess how long it will take the first time. Guesses range from an absurdly short two seconds to an absurdly long two minutes. But we don't evaluate the guesses initially, as we want to demonstrate from the start that it is okay to express ideas without fear of ridicule, particularly when none of us have any clear evidence to use for or against an idea.

Cooperative challenge games are used throughout the year to build and maintain community.

And so we play. I follow the pulse around the circle, timing it on my watch, until it returns to the starting point. Announcing the time, we laugh and cheer and reflect on our initial guesses. Then we ask for new guesses as to how much faster we might be able to pass the pulse, and we try again.

We do this a few times until the students feel they have achieved a successful level of competence. Then we talk about why they have been able to decrease the amount of time required. This debriefing allows the students to come up with conclusions about cooperation, practice, familiarity of a task, and characteristics that we can then ask them to relate to more academic tasks like writing or projects. This debriefing is a crucial part of every challenge game we play. In fact, it is part of every activity we do in Soundings. The activity alone is not sufficient to guarantee concept formulation or learning. Through directed discussion after the activity, students make connections and learn to articulate those connections. They also hear ideas from their peers, gain new perspectives, and thus internalize the lessons. Even at this game-like level, they are learning to think about actions, meanings, and consequences.

If time permits, we might play a variation of the game right away. Perhaps doing it with eyes closed, or maybe sending the pulse in the opposite direction with the correspondingly reversed sound, "peeb." If we play again, we debrief again and analyze changes in our results.

At one time or another, we will revisit this game in varied and more complex forms throughout the year, as we will most of the challenge activities we employ. By so doing, we create one more small thread of connection running through the Soundings year, while we continue to build thinking skills and to enhance our community.

Returning to the room, I give the students a 3x5 card and ask them to jot down up to five questions they would like to ask of my teaching partner or me. I tell them that they can ask anything they want, although we reserve the right to answer any honest way we want and, furthermore, that we then get to ask them a question in return. This little activity, as you might guess, serves several important purposes. First and foremost, it represents an interesting and enjoyable way for teachers and students to get to know each other. The students are eager to learn all they can about the new adults in their life; obliging them establishes a foundation of trust by example. I honor every question with an honest answer, though occasionally the most honest answer is the admission that I cannot answer a question fully and remain within the bounds of propriety. Often if a highly personal or potentially controversial question arises, I can answer it humorously in an honest way that the student does not expect. For a truly tame example, students always want to know my age; I always tell them that I'm 4.6 billion years old—a reference to the chemicals of my body that have been around since the formation of the solar system. If pressed further, I might add that I'm certainly old enough to know better than to worry about birthdays.

Clearly, we don't attempt to answer every question on the first day. We usually spend about half an hour at most on this activity and then move on. We ask the students to keep their cards, however, and we tackle a few more questions each day over the next week or so until we've exhausted the more common types of questions. Along the way, we also debrief this activity. We talk about the kinds of questions we ask and the kinds of information questions elicit. This is a subtle introduction to the theme building process soon to start that involves asking hundreds of questions.

This is also an excellent time to introduce needed listening and discussion skills. In their eagerness to ask questions and in their enthusiasm to react to responses, the students often begin to talk among themselves or out of turn. Calm and simple reminders that such actions hinder our discussion and limit our ability to proceed usually refocus the students, at least temporarily. Depending on the group, repeated reminders may be necessary while we remain patient, respectful, and resolute. Remember, we set an example through our reactions. If we raise our voices and assert adult authority, that will ultimately undermine our attempts to build the trusting relationships desired. Also remember that for most students this is a new situation. Most have never before been afforded an opportunity to relate to an adult as a relatively equal partner; so they have to learn how adults interact cooperatively. Tangentially, this is another reason why the partnered team of teachers in the same room is a valuable structure. Young adolescents see two adults working together harmoniously, even if they sometimes disagree. Consistently modeling this respectful and cooperative behavior while maintaining high expectations for the students to do the same ultimately strengthens the learning community. Once again, no activity serves only a single purpose.

Young adolescents see two adults working together harmoniously, even if they sometimes disagree.

Additional community building and orientation activities

To get everyone up and moving again after having been seated for awhile, we next introduce one of two possible activities designed to help students become familiar with their new room. The first of these is a "map the room" exercise. I give each student a 12" x 18" piece of blank white drawing paper and ask them to make themselves a map of the classroom. I instruct them to be as specific as possible. For example, I urge them not to write simply "bookshelf," but to record the types of books found on each shelf. The same goes for cabinets, closets, files, and all the nooks and crannies of the room. Then we set them loose for 10 or 15 minutes to explore and map their new world.

As we sense they are finishing, we call them all back to their seats and ask for volunteers to point out unusual things they found or something they think will be particularly useful to them during the year. Students are encouraged to add to their maps things they may not have seen or labeled. We also encourage the students to ask questions about materials or objects in the classroom. Again, through an apparently simple activity we learn a lot about our students. They, in turn, learn about the resources in the room, as well as something about careful observations and specific descriptions—two skills we will insist on in future research projects!

An alternative to mapping the room is the similar exercise "Facts-in-Five." I give the students 3x5 cards and tell them that they will have approximately five minutes to use the resources in the room to find at least two facts about the topic named. The topic doesn't really matter in and of itself, but it should certainly tie in with your larger objectives. Thus, I use this game if my opening project challenge, which I'll describe more in subsequent pages, revolves around a particular subject. For example, one year we challenged the students to design and build kites. So, in that case, we could ask the students to find facts about air currents, wind, or even the elements of flight.

The students are further instructed to record their sources and where they found those sources in the room. Then they are set loose to explore and search for facts. This gets them moving around and interacting with each other. It also gives them a directed opportunity to discover and use some of the resources in the room. When called back together, we go over some of the facts and discuss resources. Students point out where they found different types of resources, which ones proved more or less valuable, and why. We talk about the importance of carefully documenting sources of information. Again, these are all concepts and skills that will be critical as we get into more serious research later in the year. This activity introduces these notions in an enjoyable way that simultaneously serves to help build the learning community.

I can't emphasize enough, however, the importance of debriefing. While the discussion doesn't have to be drawn out or lengthy, it needs to happen. A couple of well-directed questions will help students make the connections desired, reinforce those connections, and reinforce by example the significance of thinking about one's thinking and actions. In a very real sense, these short deconstruction sessions are one of the most important parts of the teaching strategy because they affect the metacognitive skill development we are trying to encourage in

Short deconstruction sessions are one of the most important parts of the teaching strategy because they affect the metacognitive skill development we are trying to encourage.

curriculum integration. So we build them into everything we do, and I encourage all teachers to do the same.

Between these types of challenge activities and their debriefing discussions, we begin to introduce some of the structural and logistical aspects of the learning community. For example, we go through the logbook with the class and explain its content and purpose. We point out the sections of the board containing the log question, quotation, and assignments. Students copy down the first log question and the first quotation in preparation for completing responses for homework.

The logbook also contains schedules of due dates for some of the major responsibilities, such as the class log and the quotation responsibilities for the year. We review these and discuss their purpose and the requirements. We have the students highlight their name whenever it appears on each schedule. We also ask them to put the corresponding due dates on the calendar in their binder and in the assignment (agenda) book that the school provides for them.

At another point in the day, perhaps after playing another cooperative game, we turn our attention to the summer packet materials. We collect one or two of the assignments and have some students share their time lines. Then we take some time to make sure the students have correctly set up their reading journals using the forms we gave them in the summer packet. We discuss the purpose and importance of the reading journal. We go over the schedule of due dates, and each student is asked to hand in his or her journal for review.

At this time, we also ask the students to list those journal due dates in the back of their journal and assign to each a target number of entries they hope to have validated by each date. The district sets the year's target at 25 entries, so we talk to the students about planning out their year's reading to meet that goal. We mention preparing to read less during major project times or during rehearsals for the eighth-grade musical, for example, and they need to compensate for that by reading more over winter and spring vacations. Student volunteers share their targets out loud, and the class discusses them. This helps all members of the class determine more realistic reading goals, and it also ties in nicely with the upcoming discussions of goals we are about to initiate. We will check these targets when we do our first review of each journal. At that time we can conference with any student who seems to be having difficulty establishing reasonable targets.

To accomplish these reviews more easily, we divide the class alphabetically into four groups of ten. Each group hands journals in on a different week each month. As a result, my teaching partner and I each have to review just five journals a week, far from an overwhelming task. Again, these lists and due dates are predetermined and printed out over the summer, ready for the students when they arrive.

Extensive discussions and goal-setting activities launched

With some of the more structural considerations out of the way for now, we begin some of the directed discussions that continue to lay the foundation for our learning community. I like to begin by asking students to brainstorm with their table group a list of criteria for a good teacher. Specifically, I ask, "What does it take to be a good teacher?" Groups put their lists on large sheets of newsprint that we hang up around the room. From these lists we assemble a master list of the characteristics most groups think are most important. Then we repeat the process but change the question to, "What does it take to be a successful student?"

Students have many opportunities to hone their oral reading skills.

In the act of making and comparing these lists, students quickly discern commonalities. It becomes apparent that we all desire similar things for and from ourselves. With this established, conversation readily turns to questions of how we can help each other reach mutual goals.

To help structure this discussion, we return to another activity from the summer packet and to two pages in the students' logbooks. All three of these focus on setting goals. We read through the summer packet activity with the students, asking for volunteers to read aloud. I should note that this is a procedure we try to employ almost every day of our year.

WHAT MAKES A GOOD TEACHER?
(Student comments collected in Soundings I)

enthusiasm   –wanting to teach
                 –loves teaching
                 –dedication
control   –not too much or too little
                 –able to discipline a student
willing to answer questions
willing to learn from others
                   –open to new ideas
                   –asks for students' opinions
having good ideas
being committed   –willing to work hard
creativity
practicality
responsible
honest
fair
nice
caring   –likes kids
taking time to help students
                   –having the heart to help a student
                     who can sometimes be a problem
knowledgeable   –intelligent
                   –knows material being covered
understanding the students you teach
open minded
patience   –gives reasonable time for work
tolerance
respects students
                   –doesn't put people on the spot
                   –doesn't look down on students
trustworthy   –can keep students' secrets
cautious   –careful
confident   –handles stress and temper well
sets a good example
                   –hates humiliating kids
pride
sensitivity
knows right from wrong

WHAT MAKES A GOOD STUDENT?
(Student comments collected in Soundings I)

paying attention
wants to learn   −*motivated*   −*persistence*
                                      −*committed*   −*always does his/her best*
follows directions
respectful   −*able to respect boundaries made by*
                                        teachers and peers
fair to others
caring
courteous   −*listens well/attentive*
                                      −*patience*
                                      −*tolerance*
                                      −*nice*
uses appropriate language
behaves in class   −*obeys rules*
creative
enthusiasm
participating   −*giving your opinion*
                                      −*not afraid to ask questions*
                                      −*encourages others*
cooperative   −*works well in groups*
                                      −*works well with teachers*
being practical
being responsible
                                      −*doing homework and assignments*
                                      −*makes up missed work*
artistic
honest
trustworthy   −*doesn't cheat*
reflective   −*takes time to realize what*
                                        they do and don't understand
                                      −*think for yourself*
                                      −*open-minded*
understanding
organized, uses time well
speaks clearly   −*propensity not to yell*
                                      −*able to talk in front of people*
knowledgeable
good humor   −*happy, cheerful*
helpful
pride in self and work
courageous
flexible

We keep track of which students read to ensure that every student has several chances to sharpen oral reading skills. At the same time, we are thus able to gauge the students' fluency. Data on frequency and fluency of reading aloud will be reported on the mid- and end-of-year progress reviews as students address some of the district's literacy standards.

This initial reading again focuses on setting goals and gets the students to share what some of their goals are. We hear about long-range life goals, objectives for the coming year, and goals concerning extra-scholastic activities. We compare and contrast these with the characteristics we listed for successful students and discuss how they are interrelated and, indeed, often interdependent. We also talk about writing goals so that they are clear, specific, challenging, and attainable.

Based on the reading and subsequent discussion, we next ask the students to write down on the goals sheet in their logbook the several goals they feel are most important to them for their year in Soundings. We remind them that they are putting their goals in the front of their logbook because they will use that log daily and be continually reminded of their goals. We also point out that the sheet has spaces for amending goals; we will revisit initial goals several times during the year to edit and revise them according to the degree of progress each student makes toward fulfilling his or her goals.

Then we remind them that setting or writing a goal is not the whole story. To help us meet our goals, we need to think about those behaviors that will lead us in the appropriate direction. So we ask them to think about, share, and write down on the follow-up sheet in the logbook some of the actions and responsibilities they must take to help themselves and their peers achieve the goals they've set.

The reader should by now clearly sense at least two major patterns established through these activities.

1. The first is structural: almost every activity asks students to think and act more or less individually first, then to work with a small group of peers, and ultimately to share their thoughts with the class as a whole. Along the way individual ideas get revised and combined to become community ideas, which are then recorded for all to see and share.

2. The second pattern mirrors the first but specifically relates to students' thinking: we ask them to assert initial thoughts, gather additional data and apply the information to their original ideas,

reconstruct or amend the initial thoughts, and finally reassert and justify any changes or lack of changes. These two intertwined, patterned processes are at the heart of everything we do in curriculum integration; they are the very skills and understandings we in a democracy are supposed to provide our young citizens. And, of course, we also seek to develop the confidence and determination to apply these skills in debating issues and make informed decisions for the welfare of all.

I hope the reader is beginning to see that this is not merely rhetoric. If education is supposed to be all about the students, then this is a process that can make it a reality.

Obviously this process does not occur only or entirely on the first day of school. It is continually repeated and reinforced each and every day throughout the year. Indeed, though much of what has been described thus far often does occur on day one, parts of it just as frequently spill into day two, three, or even four as we mix in other activities designed to extend and enhance the foundations of the learning community. Keep in mind, however, that no activity or concept is presented in isolation. Rather, every new activity is introduced through its direct connections to what has gone before, to the concepts of goal setting, for example, or cooperative procedures, or the metacognitive processes established on day one. All aspects of the day's work, from the log question, to the challenge games, to the class discussions, are purposefully planned instructional activities designed to focus on connections, model the metacognitive process, and reinforce the democratic community through student voice, participation, and empowerment.

Selecting affirmations

Directly connected to setting individual goals, which are in turn derived from the expression and understanding of communal aspirations, is the concept of the class affirmations. Affirmations are introduced to the group as terms we would like to use—and ones we hope others would use—to describe ourselves and our work together. They should reflect our important goals and aspirations, as well as the ways we go about achieving our aims. With this in mind, we ask each student to write down at least five or six such adjectives they think they might want to use to represent their Soundings class. This can be done as a homework assignment to speed up the process. I have also accomplished this step through a log question. It can just as easily be done in class by allowing a few minutes of silence for the students to reflect and record their terms.

Whichever method is used, the students are next asked to share and discuss possible affirmations with their table group and come up with a list of the ones they agree are potentially the best from their group. After allowing time for groups to share, discuss, and determine their choices—during which time my partner and I like to circulate, listen, and ask questions requiring students to justify some of the terms they list—I call for a volunteer to write on the board or a large sheet of paper, and another to type a copy of the same record on a computer. Then we solicit a term from each table group in turn and record how many groups have the same term. We keep going around the room adding a term from each group until all the groups' terms are included on our master list.

It is important that we accept and honor all suggestions at this point. A time for debate will follow, but this is the time to make sure everyone's ideas are heard and accepted. In fact, I usually ask at this time if any individual has a term that he or she really wants on the list, but it was not selected by any of the smaller groups. If any are offered, they are added. The point here is to demonstrate to the community of students that you are truly serious about hearing everyone's voice. This level of trust is crucial to the community's ultimate level of success. Any student who feels his or her ideas have not been included will begin to feel disenfranchised,

Following the generation of possible affirmations in table groups, a lengthy initial list is compiled and the process of consolidation begins.

and cracks in the community's foundation will result—cracks that can have devastating effects later in the year.

It is not unusual to have a very lengthy list, often upward of 80 words. Obviously, this is too unwieldy a number to be workable, a fact the students quickly recognize. So I challenge them to think of a fair way to trim the list. The first suggestion is often to look for synonyms and retain only the most descriptive. This gets us into valuable discussions of *denotation* and *connotation*, terms we will employ throughout the year in our debates, our research, and our writing. It also causes students to begin to look closely at the words, examine shades of meaning critically, and reach a conclusion that best serves the community.

As we debate the meanings and power of various adjectives, some terms will fall out or rise to the top by association with other terms removed or retained. The group will deem some silly; many will require a trip to the dictionary to verify or clarify the definition; some will have a potentially negative connotation or undesirable interpretation. Such terms will eventually get removed through discussion and consensus, though sometimes only after serious debate. Often this discussion and paring process occurs gradually, a little every day, over a week or so. True democracy takes time, discussion, and reflection.

Sometimes we get lucky and the group arrives through consensus at a workable list of 8 to 12 terms. Sometimes we can't seem to get below 20. When this occurs, I challenge the class for suggestions as to ways we can equitably resolve the problem. This inevitably brings up the suggestion of a majority vote, which provides a wonderful opportunity to discuss issues such as the difference between consensus and majority rule, the potential tyranny of the majority, the nature of democracy. Again, what more important issues can young adolescents living in a democratic society discuss?

Eventually, the class looks for consensus. Sometimes this involves open compromises and tradeoffs among factions promoting certain terms. Sometimes it ends with everyone ranking all the terms individually and tallying the scores each term receives to eliminate those that no one gives high scores. There is no one right way, though there are wrong ways; and the process is more important than the outcome. The affirmations chosen by the first six Soundings classes follow.

Once the list has been finalized, the students are asked to write up full definitions for two of the affirmations as a homework assignment. They draw one word out of a hat to ensure that all the words are defined at least four times, and then they self-select a second word to define. The definition may come from a dictionary or be in the student's own words. Both forms are valid for the discussions that will follow. However, beyond the definition, the student is required to include a description of how someone would recognize that affirmation being embodied in the classroom. This forces them to think about the adjective in concrete terms of behaviors, which will be important in self-assessment and recognition procedures throughout the year.

Soundings I (1998–1999)	Soundings II (1999–2000)	Soundings III (2001–2002)
Committed	Adventurous	Aspiring
Cooperative	Creative	Cooperative
Creative	Democratic	Creative
Motivated	Diligent	Enthusiastic
Respectful	Enthusiastic	Exemplary
Responsible	Unique	Intelligent
		Respectful
		Responsible
Soundings IV (2002–2003)	**Soundings V** (2003–2004)	**Soundings VI** (2004–2005)
Confident	Confident	Ambitious
Curious	Cooperative	Awesome
Enthusiastic	Creative	Bold
Humorous	Honest	Creative
Independent	Intelligent	Determined
Motivated	Optimistic	Enthusiastic
Responsible	Responsible	Genuine
Unique	Unique	Optimistic
		Trustworthy
		Vivacious

The next day we read definitions aloud and discuss the examples. This sharing allows the class to refine their definitions and clarify their ideas of ways to assess their performance with respect to the affirmations. It further allows them a chance to modify and edit their written definitions and descriptions before turning in the final version that will be included in our affirmations book. This book will be on display in the classroom at all times. With all the definitions and descriptions, it will serve as a ready resource at times when the class needs to discuss successes or perhaps even lapses in living up to our affirmations. In addition, we ask for volunteers to design artistic renderings of each affirmation to use as illustrations in the book. The best of these are selected by the class for painting on the wall to replace those of last year's class.

Developing our community guidelines

With our goals and our affirmations now determined, it is time to formalize our guidelines for the classroom. We don't start the year with a predetermined list of rules, other than the general school regulations in the student handbook; nor do we initiate this discussion until we have completed the work thus far described. There are at least two reasons for this. First, the foregoing discussions of goals and affirmations, along with the ongoing cooperative challenge activities, establish the foundation and the context students will need if they are to design a functional set of democratic guidelines. Second, the students need to spend some time in the Soundings classroom adjusting to working with the same group and experiencing the community in order to understand what steps they will need to take to ensure that community's continued success.

Having had discussions in determining personal goals and community affirmations, it is now an easy and necessary step to move the discussion in the direction of community guidelines. The students are beginning to feel as though they are part of a real community. They have been learning to work together through games, discussions, and whatever initial mini-project we have chosen to get them started. They are beginning to see where potential problems could arise, and they are ready and able now to think through strategies to lessen or avoid difficulties.

We introduce this step in terms of a bill of rights—not a list of rules. We know what we all want and need to be successful: we know what it takes to be a successful student and teacher; we have our affirmations and our personal goals. Now, what guidelines do we need to establish to ensure we all get the maximum opportunity to achieve our goals?

Once again, we pose that question to individuals first, either as a homework assignment or a log question. Individual responses come to the table groups for consensus; then table groups present ideas to the class. Lists are generated and debated. The class eventually agrees on the basic framework and what needs to be included. Then we turn over the task of drafting a bill of rights to a small committee of volunteers. This committee is given work time to hammer out a preliminary document, type it up, and submit it to the class. More discussion and debate follows; the committee takes suggestions and reworks the document accordingly. It usually takes two drafts, sometimes three, to come up with a final version the class agrees includes everything they want in wording they like. Two examples from different years follow.

SOUNDINGS II
Bill of Rights

We the people of the second SOUNDINGS class, in order to form a perfect environment, establish rules, ensure domestic tranquility, provide for everyone's needs, promote the general welfare, and secure the blessings of learning for ourselves, do ordain and establish this Bill of Rights for the second SOUNDINGS class.

RIGHT I

Soundings shall make no rule that in any way inhibits any certain person from being democratic. All should be able to vote, to disagree on any subject, to express one's own opinion. Each person should have the right to stand up for his or her beliefs.

RIGHT II

Soundings shall make no rule prohibiting fulfillment of any person's needs: including needs to be one's own individual, to get help when needed, to know how one is progressing, and to know when his or her responsibilities are due. There is also to be no prohibition against a person's need to be a leader or a follower. Every person's ideas will and should be considered. All persons shall have the right to have things explained clearly.

RIGHT III

Soundings shall make no rule denying one's personal respect. All shall have the right to expect others to be friendly, and to be treated like an adult.

RIGHT IV

Soundings shall make no rule that in any way prohibits a student's ability to learn. Each person will have the right to learn in a safe and healthy environment. This requires cooperation, equal participation on everyone's part, and the ability for all persons to ask questions.

(Ratified October 1999)

SOUNDINGS V
Class Charter

As members of the fifth SOUNDINGS class, from the year 2003 to 2004, we create this constitution to form a better community, ensure the opportunity to succeed, keep the peace between students and teachers, and secure the rights and freedoms of every SOUNDINGS member; and so we do establish this document for the SOUNDINGS community.

On Responsibilities

All SOUNDINGS constituents have the responsibility to do their best and try their hardest to succeed. With privileges come responsibilities, and every SOUNDINGS member is in charge of fulfilling them. All of the members must comply with every responsibility. All students must ask questions, perform their own work, complete their logbook, listen to others, raise their hand before speaking, be creative, clean up after themselves, make their own decisions, remind classmates of their responsibilities, and most importantly not abuse the rights and privileges given to them in SOUNDINGS.

On Privileges

By carrying out the above responsibilities, SOUNDINGS students are given certain privileges that must be taken care of in order to have a peaceful year. The predominant privileges in SOUNDINGS are those of a democratic society: deciding what we learn, speaking our mind, being creative and going out on a limb, learning, playing the ever-popular game of buttball, and the overall privilege of the SOUNDINGS experience.

On Rights

The rights of every SOUNDINGS member shall not be abused, but taken positive advantage of and used to their full power to ensure equality, fairness, and a great learning experience for the class. The rights granted to the class are:
  – to ask any and every appropriate question that comes to mind
  – to be creative and take "risks" to learn
  – to speak our mind, within appropriate bounds
  – to have our opinions and views heard
  – to receive and offer criticism in a constructive and appropriate manner
  – to be respected by our teachers and our fellow students
  – to know our work will be respected by our peers
  – to utilize the facilities when it is necessary
  – to eat in the classroom, at lunchtime, and during class, as long as it doesn't disrupt class activities
  – to learn.   (Ratified October 2003)

The reader will note how these documents assert guidelines and expectations, but do so in a positive and affirming manner. The emphasis is on what should be done, rather than on what should not be done. Furthermore, since the guidelines came from the students, they have ownership of them and are likely to live up to them. As Mike, one of my students, said: "Since we determined these guidelines, I feel that this is the most fair and just school environment that I've ever been part of." When students begin to trust that the environment is indeed "fair and just," they begin to want to maintain that milieu and are willing to remind each other of mutual responsibilities and expectations throughout the year.

Using this approach and process is the main reason we have almost no discipline problems in Soundings. Treating students with respect, expecting them to do the same, enabling them to come to an understanding of the importance of certain guidelines, and then empowering them to articulate those guidelines eliminates all the problems associated with forcing an externally derived set of rules upon individuals. Isn't that the very foundation of a democratic society— governance of the people by the people? As one student, Michelle, put it: "Our classroom is a democratic classroom because we each have different views and opinions, and we aren't afraid to share them. At the same time, we don't hold anything against a fellow student just because he/she has an opinion that we don't particularly like." Or, as Michelle's classmate Jonathan said, "A democratic classroom is a place where you can express your feelings and state your opinion without getting ridiculed." What better way can this concept be taught than by purposefully and conscientiously living it in the classroom?

The Bill of Rights, once ratified by the class, gets printed up for all to keep in their logbooks. It also goes in the front of our Affirmation Book. Some years, the class has mounted a copy on poster board, had everyone sign it, and then displayed it in the room in a prominent spot.

How will students assess their progress?

One last major document needs to be developed as a part of both the community building process and the academic process (as if the two can be separated). Though we do not use grades, we nonetheless have a compact with the parents and the students to assess each individual's progress. Consequently, we need to create an assessment form. As with the Bill of Rights, the creation of this document cannot be done effectively in the first days of school. It is better to wait until students have a couple of weeks' worth of experience in the community so they have a more realistic idea of what an assessment instrument should convey.

The first thing we discuss as we begin this process, of course, is, why do we need an assessment document, and what should it convey? The log question again serves as a good avenue for initiating this discussion, but it can also be raised directly in discussion. Either way, the process begins again with individual ideas shared and combined in small groups. Sharing group results, we develop a list of the kinds of information the students think could and should be communicated. Here is a sample list of topics generated by Soundings I.

SOUNDINGS I
Preliminary Assessment Ideas

1. Describe work in progress/topics.
2. Describe contributions to discussions.
3. Affirmations—how you've achieved or used; give examples.
4. Were you prepared?
5. Goals set for next week?
6. Living up to last goals; what do you need to do better?
7. Describe your attitude and behavior.
8. What did you achieve or accomplish?
9. How were your time management skills?
10. How organized have you been?
11. Which quote did you relate to most?
12. How well did you pay attention?
13. Were you respectful?
14. Were your ideas used?
15. Was your homework complete?
16. Did you work well with others or in a group?
17. With whom did you work well?
18. Did you attempt extra tasks beyond those required?
19. Did you give your best effort?
20. Describe something you learned.
21. Describe something you enjoyed? Or did not enjoy?
22. Parent and teacher comments.

23. Student's summary comments; how do you think you're doing?

24. Work toward long-term goal?

25. Reading Journal progress.

26. Writing and communication skills: used, learned, improved, need work.

27. Research skills: used, learned, improved, need work.

28. Listening skills: used, learned, improved, need work.

29. Technology skills: used, learned, improved, need work.

30. Artistic skills: used, learned, improved, need work.

31. Balancing academic and social issues.

Each Soundings class comes up with a similar list. The reader will agree that everything on this list is worthy of inclusion on an assessment document, which proves that students do know what is important in assessing their learning. Now the trick is to take all these possible topics and fit them on a single sheet of paper (both sides) in a format that will be user friendly but fully informative for all parties involved.

This can be accomplished in many ways. One way is to facilitate a class discussion about organizing the listed aspects into categories of related skills or content. Table groups can suggest categories and then have the class reach a consensus on the most suitable and effective categories. As students debate these categories, they are learning several important things. First, they are refining their definitions of the skills and areas to be assessed. This helps when we determine specific rubrics later on. In addition, they are strengthening the bonds of the community through this honing of a shared vision. They are also learning how to organize seemingly disparate materials or concepts into meaningful patterns and relationships. These higher-level thinking skills are the essence

In table groups, the class tackles the task of developing assessment categories.

of understanding and have direct carryover into any area of study we later pursue.

Once the major categories are determined, table groups usually take responsibility for different categories and suggest effective methods or formats for assessing their categories. These suggestions are then presented to the class as a whole for acceptance or modification. Once again, the discussions prove interesting and beneficial on many levels. As a teacher, it has always interested me to note how adept at effective discussion the students are becoming by this time.

Ultimately, we call for a committee of volunteers, as we did with our Bill of Rights, to take all the agreed-upon suggestions and draft a prototype for our assessment document. We then follow the same peer editing and revision process until we have a document we can all agree conveys the necessary information in a way that is both meaningful and practical. Every year's document looks a little different, but they have many features in common. Two examples follow of what the forms have looked like over the years.

Soundings 　　　　**Weekly Self-Assessment Sheet** 　　　　**1998–99**

Name: _____ 　　　　Date: _____

I. Affirmations:

Motivated　　Cooperative　　Creative　　Committed　　Responsible　　Respectful

Choose at least two and give a specific example of how you followed your affirmations.

II. Behaviors: (check appropriate response) *exceptional, acceptable, not acceptable*

My behavior this week can best be described as:

My attitude toward my peers was:

My attitude toward my work was:

My attitude toward the program was:

My effort this week can best be described as:

My participation in discussions was:

My participation in group/class activities was:

My cooperation was:

---

continued

III. Skills: (check appropriate response) *exceptional, acceptable, not acceptable*

My research work was:

My written work was:

My organization was:

My time management was:

My preparation was:

IV. I owe the following assignments: _____

_____

V. This week I learned:_____

_____

VI. My top accomplishments this week included: _____

_____

_____

VII. My goal for the coming week is: _____

_____

VIII. How did I accomplish last week's goal?_____

_____

_____

IX. I added _____ new books to my reading journal this week.

X. Overall I am   pleased   not pleased (circle one) with my work this week

because:_____

_____

Student's Additional Comments: (optional)

Student Signature: _____

Teacher Comment:

Teacher Signature: _____

Parent Comment:

Parent Signature: _____   Date: _____

Soundings V, 2003–2004

Self-Assessment Form   Name:_____   Date:_____

Summary: Describe what you have learned and what important activities we have done in the past two weeks.

Responsibilities   Circle the appropriate response.
<u>Log Book</u>

Log Question Completion	always	mostly	generally	rarely	never
Daily Summary Completion	always	mostly	generally	rarely	never
Goals Completion	always	mostly	generally	rarely	never
Quote Response Completion	always	mostly	generally	rarely	never
Quality of Entries	thorough		mostly thorough		not thorough
	consistent		mostly consistent		not consistent
	organized		mostly organized		not organized

<u>Spelling Book</u>

Use of Current Words	often	sometimes	rarely	never
Completion	always	mostly	rarely	never
Completes on Time	always	mostly	rarely	never
Participates in Review	always	mostly	rarely	never

<u>Reading Journal</u>

Completion	always	mostly	rarely	never
Format of Entries	varied	similar	identical	
Creativeness of Entries	very	somewhat	not	
Neatness of Entries	very	somewhat	not	

Number of Entries completed: _____   Target for Next Time: _____
Title of Current Book: _____

Group Work: Give examples of your level of group work in the last two weeks.
Individual Skills: Indicate where you feel you have been for the past two weeks. You may also include comments.
Organization: very organized----------------somewhat organized----------------not organized
Time Management managed well----------managed okay---------------needs improvement
Effort: strong effort--------------------------- okay effort------------------needs improvement

continued

Choose one affirmation and describe how you have exhibited it in the past two weeks OR describe how you will meet it in the next two weeks.

Goals:

On what goals have you progressed? How have you progressed?

On what do you want to improve before the next self-assessment?

Teacher Comments:

_____
Teacher Signature

Parent Comments:

_____
Parent Signature

_____
Student Initials

Date: _____

By now it is about the first week in October, time for the first self-assessments to go home to parents as promised. The first time assessments go home, we include a cover letter (p. 57) and a second copy of the scheduled dates previously sent home. The letter explains how students created the assessment document, and it reminds them of the parents' responsibilities to go over the document with their child before signing it and making any comment. The letter also asks for feedback on the document. It is, after all, a living document that can be and often is changed as we find ways to improve it. The parents clearly have a vested interest in the success and effectiveness of this form, so their perspectives and suggestions can only serve to strengthen it. In addition to this letter, we now send an e-mail notice letting parents know the letter is coming home.

This same process will be revisited at least two more times during the year, to create the midyear and end-of-year progress review documents. Because these documents employ rubrics and tend to be about 15 or 16 pages long, the students go into even more depth in their discussions when designing these self-assessment forms. By midyear, and certainly by the end of the year, they have become very skilled at determining and articulating assessment information. Ultimately, the two lengthy documents look much alike, with only minor adjustments related to the time of year. For example, at midyear students often discuss plans for the second half of the year, but this obviously does not apply at the end of the year. Copies of the year-end progress review can be found in Appendix 4 (p. 182).

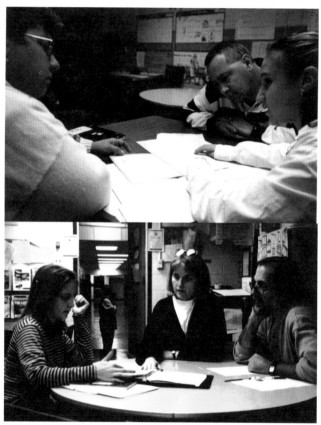

Students have two opportunities to plan and conduct student-led conferences.

Students plan and conduct student-led conferences, first in November and again in May. This form of assessment and accountability gives students genuine ownership of their own education and a leadership experience. Parents, universally, find these conferences to be meaningful.

As is the case with reading journal reviews and logbook checks, we don't try to do everyone's self-assessment at the same time. That would take too long and limit our abilities to pay close attention to each one. With our 40 students, we have found it best to divide the class in half alphabetically and have each half complete its self-assessments on alternating weeks. Most weeks we have the students fill out the self-assessment during advisory time on Tuesday morning. We avoid Mondays for several reasons, but mostly because there are a number of Monday holidays during the year. In addition, the students tend to be back into their work mode by Tuesdays and have a firmer grasp on what they are doing and what they need to do.

SOUNDINGS

An Integrative Program for Eighth Graders

Radnor Middle School
131 South Wayne Avenue
Wayne, PA 19087   October __, 200_

Dear SOUNDINGS Parents:

Today you are receiving the first of your child's biweekly progress reports. This form was cooperatively developed by the students and teachers in SOUNDINGS as a way to communicate with you on a regular basis. It is a work in progress, so we welcome your comments and suggestions as we seek ways to refine and improve the form and the process.

Since this is the first time, let us review for you how this process is designed to work:

1. Roughly every other Tuesday morning the students will fill out the weekly assessment form and hand it in to us.

   [Note: See schedule for your child's assessment dates. We will make every effort to let you know of changes due to unforeseen conditions, such as weather or trips.]

2. We will divide the papers between us, review them, write our brief comments on them, photocopy them, and send them home to you with your student on the following Wednesday afternoon.

3. The students have been instructed to share with you this assessment form, along with their Daily Log Book, their Reading Journal, and their work folder Wednesday evening. Together, these materials should give you a clear picture of what and how your student is doing in SOUNDINGS.

4. A space has been provided on the form for you to make any comments or ask any questions you may have.

   Comments are not required, but we do ask that you **sign** the form to verify that you have had the opportunity to review it and the other materials with your student.

5. The student returns the signed form to us on Thursday morning and transfers finished work from the work folder to his/her file folders.

We hope you'll find this process informative, helpful, and fairly unobtrusive. Again, we welcome any questions or comments you may have. As always, you can also reach us at 610-386-6300 ext. 6437.

Thank you in advance for your help in making SOUNDINGS a successful learning experience for your student.

Mark Springer   Mary Canniff

After the students complete the form, my teaching partner and I divide the 20 evenly between us. Then we read over each one, make both margin comments and a fuller statement in the allotted space, and photocopy the document. We return them to the students on Wednesday to go home Wednesday evening. Ideally the forms are returned with a parent's signature and usually a comment on Thursday morning. At that time, we keep the signed original and give the student the photocopy to store in his or her self-assessment portfolio. That way the student will have copies of all the assessments when it comes time for student-led conferences, and the parents get a file of all assessments in June as a record of the entire year.

Both students and parents alike generally appreciate this form of assessment communication far more than the traditional letter grades and report cards with a menu of little numbered comments. Sara expressed the sentiments of most of her peers when she said, "I like having self-assessments because I don't get compared to other students' best; I get compared to my best."

By now the reader must be wondering if all we do is sit around and talk in groups or in class. At times it probably seems that way to us, too. However, these discussion activities are broken up frequently with other activities. For example, we introduce new cooperative challenges almost every day, as well as variations on some of the more popular ones. We start painting our affirmations on the wall, begin decorating the doors with a student-selected motif, and work on the initial class project.

The initial class project

This initial class project, first referred to earlier when discussing the "Facts-in-Five" game we sometimes play on day one, is introduced very early in the year, usually on the first or second day of school. It is designed by the teachers to introduce a number of important concepts that we will use throughout the year. First and foremost, this project builds community and cooperation skills. In addition, it has a problem-solving component that requires planning and organization as well as a research component. It always has a tangible end product that involves some effort by each individual, by small groups, and by the class as a whole. Needless to add, it provides fun, too.

The first year of Soundings, I bought a relatively inexpensive roll of 8-mil clear plastic sheeting. The plastic, when unrolled and unfolded, was ten feet wide by several hundred feet long. I cut two 30-foot lengths of this plastic and laid them out on the floor of our activity center, a remodeled old gym that the school uses for many large group purposes. Then Sheila, my partner, and I challenged the class to work together to construct a freestanding ten-foot cube.

The first thing the students had to do was come up with a plan and a course of action. They quickly decided that they would need some additional materials—duct tape, scissors, a meter stick, and a large fan. Further discussion resulted in a decision to ask for a little more plastic to build a sleeve for attaching the fan to the cube. So we gave them duct tape, scissors, a meter stick, a 20-inch box fan, and another 10-foot square of plastic.

On their own, they formed small groups to tackle different parts of the project. One group made the sleeve and attached it to the fan. Other groups measured and taped different edge seams. Then they had to merge everyone's efforts to hold up the cube while final edges were sealed and the sleeve attached to one face of the cube.

The entire process to this point took several hours, spread out over three days. Remember, we were also conducting our various discussions and playing other challenge games throughout this same period. On the third day we were ready to turn on the fan and test our creation. A group cheer arose

Experimenting with a way to put the cube together.

from 42 beaming faces as the cube inflated. I admit it didn't look like a perfect cube, more like a cross between a cube and a globe. Nevertheless, it was marvelous, and the class bonded around the sense of communal accomplishment.

But we weren't finished.

While flush with our success, we challenged the class to work in small groups to design and build a number of smaller, inflatable shapes that we could then attach to our quasi-cube to construct a single, unified structure they could all move around in, much like those "habitrail" things made for hamsters and mice to play in, only on a much larger human scale. We discussed how we could most effectively do this. I told them how much plastic was left, and that we would provide more tape but could buy no more plastic. The students decided that we needed to avoid wasting plastic, so we should make paper models first. We gave them sheets of graph paper to establish sizes and make patterns.

Groups formed, and they worked out a variety of possible shapes. They experimented with sizes and seams, and they discussed ways to attach shapes together. Once workable models had been made to scale, the groups set about dividing up the remaining plastic and constructing their respective shapes.

We had different sized pyramids, mini-cubes, and tube-like structures, but my favorite was a donut-like ring large enough to easily crawl through. The students even spray-painted icing and sprinkles on it.

Again, this process, worked in among discussions and other activities, took another week or so. Then we put all the shapes together, added a couple of more box fans to facilitate inflation, and watched our human-habitrail rise from the gym floor. We celebrated this latest success by getting inside, signing the walls with markers, and taking lots of photos. Then we debriefed the entire process and discussed what we had learned from it about cooperation, planning, and teamwork. We also discussed diversity and how all the different ideas and different shapes had come together to make a cohesive whole that was greater than an individual part. Finally, we talked about how we could use all these concepts in our subsequent work.

Proud students relax in front of their created habitrail.

Another year my teaching partner and I chose parachutes as an opening theme. We used the idea that "a mind is like a parachute—it works best when open" as an early quotation, and we challenged groups to design and construct parachutes that would be able to lower a plastic cup filled with marbles to the ground without crashing or spilling the marbles. Students could use any materials they wanted and make the chute any size up to a maximum of four feet in diameter. They also had to devise a way to attach the chute to the cup.

Groups tried all types of designs. When initial attempts failed to work as they had hoped, the students quickly turned to the Internet and began on their own to research parachute design. This led to new designs that fared much better in test drops from a rolling ladder platform we borrowed from the maintenance department.

When the chutes were finally ready, we took them outside. A volunteer from each group accompanied me up the two-story fire escape, where we put marbles into the cup and dropped the chutes to the ground. The group decided how many marbles they wanted in the cup, and students on the ground kept a record of the number each chute held on each drop, and the results of the descent. This allowed us, during the debriefing, to discuss experimental design, the need for research and planning, careful observation techniques, and record keeping, along with the other lessons learned about teamwork.

In the sixth year of Soundings, we took advantage of the fact that our school district was in the process of planning to construct a new middle school. Along with several other teachers, I had been invited to discuss planning concepts with the architect before the designing actually began so he could better match his forms to our functions. As we talked, and as he learned about the students' role in curriculum integration, the architect expressed an interest in getting suggestions from the students. That was all I needed to hear—I knew we had our initial project—to design a new middle school, using a combination of the architect's specifications and the students' perspectives.

The students were excited by the prospect of having input into the new building. Along with our discussions of what it takes to be a successful teacher and student, we discussed what is required in a successful middle school building. We listed areas and functions; we debated necessities versus niceties—an Olympic swimming pool and an IMAX would be wonderful, but probably not in the district's budget. We also discussed how the design of the building could affect learning on many different levels, from flexibility of activities to flow of traffic and noise in the hallways.

Once we had concept areas determined, such as the media center, the cafeteria, the auditorium, regular classrooms, and classrooms for our three integrated programs, different table groups volunteered to research and design each area. They looked at the specifications the architect had been given, and they tried to meet those requirements while also coming up with a design they thought would best fulfill the needs of those who would be using the respective areas. We worked out a standard scale so all the plans would be relative to one another, and we talked a little about drawing techniques they would need to effectively represent their ideas in a blueprint form.

The architect, who had studied the students' designs and suggestions, explains the model of the new middle school.

When all the designs were finished, each group presented its area to the class. They justified their plans, answered questions, and took suggestions from the class. Then I sent all the plans to the architect, and we moved on to our own theme planning. A number of weeks later, the architect visited and spent several hours in the Soundings classroom. He returned their designs, asking each group to again summarize its major ideas; and then he gave them feedback on how closely their ideas fit with the actual preliminary design of the building. He shared those initial blueprints with the class, along with a scale model, and the students could see firsthand how they had had an impact on the new building.

We also had a chance to hear the architect discuss the entire design process and how it compares to any other creative activity, such as writing an essay or painting a picture. The students saw how working adults use the very same skills they were using. As a result, their efforts were validated on several levels, and we were able to refer to this process throughout our year. It became one more common thread running through the year and linking the Soundings community together.

The reader should by now see how we attempt to interrelate everything in Soundings. Each step of the process is reflected in other steps and gets revisited many times in many ways, thus allowing students numerous opportunities to internalize the messages contained within the process as well as the content.

Nevertheless, I can imagine many readers saying to themselves, "But it's the beginning of October, and they haven't touched content yet." I hear this from visitors, too, and from audiences when I make presentations. I think they miss a couple of key points. First of all, the process is the content in a very real sense. The students are learning how to learn, which is very different from and much more important than memorizing facts, particularly at the middle level, often our last best chance to keep young minds engaged.

The process is the content in a very real sense. The students are learning how to learn.

Furthermore, we need to keep in mind the significance of a strong foundation. The premise here is that front-end loading pays dividends exponentially down the road. An old television advertisement for motor oil used to show a grease-smeared mechanic who, turning from fixing an engine, wiped his hands, held up a can of the oil, and advised: "You can pay me now, or pay me later." The same is true with education.

I've also had numerous skeptical teachers say, "I tried cooperative learning activities or planning with students, or giving students choices, but it just didn't work. The students couldn't do it." Invariably when I probe, I find out that they tried these activities without adequately preparing the students. If students had never been in school, I believe that they would probably take naturally to such activities; but I contend that schools teach such skills out of students. Instead, we teach individualized competition and greed; we teach students not to share knowledge and information because somehow that will give others an advantage; we teach them to fear and distrust each other. How then can we expect them suddenly to cooperate if we don't consciously and purposefully re-teach them how to do so?

My experience has clearly shown me that when we do take the time to lay the foundations properly, the students then exceed expectations for the remainder of the year. I think you'll see in the coming theme descriptions just how much more Soundings students achieve than their peers in conventional classrooms; we don't lose time later in the year trying to undo damage previously done in order to motivate students or to get them to do work they have no vested interest in doing.

One of my students, Susan H., put it this way:

> *At the beginning of the year, our work was going so slowly that I was afraid that we would not be able to keep up with the curriculum the rest of the eighth grade was learning. Now I see we were just having trouble adjusting to the kind of brainwork that Soundings required us to do. Soundings requires us to go beyond the safe zone and probe where no one has dared to go before.*

Susan's observation that she and her peers were "having trouble adjusting to the kind of brainwork" is a mature and sophisticated testament to her growing metacognition; at the same time it points to the severity of the problem in conventional curriculum.

The preliminary work I have been describing takes time to do correctly and thoroughly, but it is absolutely essential to establish and maintain the kind of learning community that will meet the real needs of young adolescents and make curriculum integration successful. Going through the community building activities is not a separate curriculum piece; it is, in fact, an integral part of planning with students. We need to think in terms of the whole complex system and not expect pieces of it to work adequately if isolated from the others. And now we're ready to apply what we have been learning to the planning of our themes for the year.

*The message is in the medium—
the content is in the process.*

CHAPTER FIVE

The Community in Action: Determining Themes for the Year

I wish sometimes that we could just jump into everything instead of spending so much time discussing everything, but in the long run it is better that we discuss everything first. —Sarah K.

Having established a firm sense of community, and having already engaged the students in activities that model the planning process, we are ready by late September to begin planning our themes. We have already employed a number of strategies involving the use and discussion of questions such as the questioning of the teachers on day one, for example. There is also a page in the summer packet devoted to a question-making activity (copy in Appendix 2) that we go over in class prior to beginning the theme building process.

Another activity we like to use challenges the students to think about questions as ways to link ideas. We give each table group a large sheet of poster board and ask them to draw a picture of a pencil or similar simple object in the middle of the space. Using this as a focus, they brainstorm as many questions as they can, and connect related questions, much like an idea web used to plan an essay or story. Groups share their webs, and we look for similarities and differences. This allows us to see the many ways questions can interrelate, as well as how one question can lead us to a virtually limitless number of other questions.

We then hammer this last point home by asking students to develop a series of at least eight questions that can link two apparently unlike topics.

Each question must flow logically from its predecessor. For example, I might start with *coffee* and ask the students to get to the Constitution of the United States. Of course, there is no one right way to do this, though there are many wrong ways that don't fit the established criteria. This example might go something like this:

- When and where was coffee first cultivated?

- When and where did coffee cultivation become commercialized for consumption beyond the farmer?

- How did the commercialization of coffee affect the economy in regions where it was grown and sold?

- Who controlled commercialized coffee production and its financial effects?

- How did the governments of the regions try to regulate the commercialization of coffee?

- How does our government regulate the cultivation, sale, or consumption of coffee?

- What gives our government the power to regulate the cultivation, sale, or consumption of coffee?

- What other aspects of daily American life does the Constitution give our government the power to regulate?

Students come up with lots of different ways to do this. This example made connections through economic and political avenues. Others have gone through questions related to health and nutrition. Still others have linked the topics of coffee and our Constitution through advertising, farming techniques, and popular culture icons like the coffeehouse milieu of the television series "Friends." Regardless of the specific outcome, the point is made that questions interconnect, and knowledge is not made up of discrete or unrelated facts—the way schools often make it seem. Furthermore, this demonstrates how we will be able to find logical ways to use everyone's questions in our theme building process.

The process is launched

The actual process now begins as we ask students to write down a list of questions they have about either themselves or the world beyond themselves. Arguments can be made for starting with questions they have about themselves as those are most closely linked with the student. But the point can also be made that students are more willing to start with less personal questions. I have started both ways in different years and have found no marked difference. The important point is to have students come to the table with an actual list of questions specifically directed toward one of the two areas, self or world.

We don't collect or read these individual lists, though we check to see that each student has one before moving to the next step. Students then share the lists with their table groups, with each student controlling which of his or her questions to divulge. Some will want to read their entire list; others will choose to share only some of the questions; still others will elect to offer only those that are similar to ones put forward by others. All are acceptable, for the goal is to generate a list of questions that two or more people at the table have in common. The questions don't have to be worded exactly the same way, but the gist of the questions should be essentially the same. For example, one student might ask why his older brother is a better athlete than he is, and another student may wonder why she can't write as well as her friends. The table group might list these as similar in the form of "Why do people have different talents or abilities?"

It is important to circulate from table to table during this activity. We often ask clarifying questions to make sure all understand what someone is asking, but we avoid making any suggestions or any attempt to push questions in any given direction. Usually, if I speak, I'll say something like, "This is what I hear you saying, John; is that what you meant?" This gives John a chance to hear how his point came across to a listener and the opportunity to rephrase it or to correct any misinterpretation.

By modeling this behavior at each table, we demonstrate several things to the entire group: (1) that we are interested in and are paying close attention to their ideas, which validates the ideas and honors the speaker; (2) that it is all right to ask for clarification, and that asking is not

Table groups discuss their individual questions and record common ones on large sheets of newsprint.

criticizing; (3) that all of us should be listening and questioning in the same respectful way; and (4) that speakers need to think carefully about what they are saying and make comments as clearly as they can. Students pick up on all of these points and begin to emulate them, particularly since we have discussed these in previous activities, conversations, and debriefing sessions. If any individual student seems to be having trouble behaving civilly, this is a good opportunity to point that out gently in a small group setting; but this is rarely necessary.

Table groups continue to discuss their individual questions and record common ones on large sheets of newsprint we pass out. We ask each group to select a recorder, to label one sheet "Self" or "World" depending on the starting prompt, and also to put the names of everyone in the group at the top of the sheet. Once table groups have assembled their list of common questions on the large sheets, a volunteer spokesperson for each group reads the list of questions out loud to the class. Then the lists are posted around the room for all to see.

This same process is next repeated using the second prompt: if students started with asking questions concerning self, they now list questions about the world beyond themselves; if they started with world questions, they now address self questions. We share in small groups and list common questions again, then report out to the whole class and post all results.

It is not unusual by this stage to have hundreds of questions now listed on papers posted around the room. What follows are the original lists compiled from all the table groups' sheets with only exact duplicates deleted.

The Individual or Self Questions from Soundings I

Who will be "the" girl for me?

What does the future have in store?

What are friends? True friends?

What is love?

Will I be successful in life?

Am I making the right decisions in life?

Is there really a Santa Claus?

Is there a god?

What will we be studying in Soundings?

Is there an afterlife?

What happens when you die?

When was the beginning of time?

Will I live a full and prosperous life?

World peace: will it happen?
How can I help make it happen?

What will result from the Presidential scandal?

Will Bill get the boot? (impeached)

---

continued

When/how will I die? Why do people die?

What kind of life do I want to live?

What can I do to make this world better?

Will I be a father/husband?

What college will I go to?

Will I ever be a Navy Seal?

Will anyone close to me become sick
or even die?

How can I prevent terrorists?

How will friendships change through the years?

What will high school and college be like?

How will my health and well-being turn out?

Will uniforms be in our school?

Will cloning affect us?

Will divorces occur in my family?

Will aliens affect us?

How will technology affect our lives?

Will technology take over our jobs and lives?

What jobs will we have?

Will I be successful?

Will I be wealthy or poor?

Will I be famous?

How will my children's health be?

Will homeless people find homes?

Will there be another war?

Will there ever be a world war three?

Will SOUNDINGS be successful?

Will people be racist or against religions?

Will there be a cure for cancer and AIDS?

Will there ever be a woman president?

How can we help people less fortunate than us?

What's the purpose of life?

Is the environment okay?

Why aren't people doing more to help the
environment?

What is my future?

Will I move? Where?

Why can't people be treated as equal?

Why is there racism and prejudice?

Why is there so much violence in schools?
Will it stop? What can we do about it?

Will there ever be a cure for diseases? AIDS?

Will anything bad ever happen to me?

What will our life be like in the future?

Why do I worry so much?

Why am I so scared of things?

What do my friends think of me?

Will I be happy in life?

Why do we fall for peer pressure?

Why do people do bad things in the world?

Why do we care what others think?

Will we all be friends in life?

How long will we live?

Will our children be good people?

Will we be good parents?

Why do we grow up?

Why are some people so mean?

Why do people tease others?

Why is life so confusing?

Why is life so stressful at times?

What will I be when I grow up?

Will I be president?

Where do babies come from?

Do wishes ever come true?

Are we alone?…The truth is out there!

Am I really a good person?

Will I ever be beautiful?

What will I look like when I'm older?

Will I ever meet people from my past?

What do I love most about life?

continued

Will I ever fall in love?	Why can't people think for themselves—dressing—concern about weight and height—drugs—peer pressure?
If I had to give up one thing, what would it be?	
Will I be the source of my family's income?	Will there always be terrorism, violence, and murder?
What will my high school reunion be like?	Will I ever win a famous prize? Nobel Peace, Miss America, Emmy, etc.?
What will the best part of our life be?	
Will I ever be cloned?	Would you be able to see your life after your death?
If reincarnation happens, what will I be?	
Will I ever be frozen (cryogenics)?	Will I still have the same friends when I'm older?
Will people ever build a community in space?	
Will people ever build a community in water? Underground?	Will I invent things? medicines? Or will other doctors and scientists?
Will the Titanic ever be recovered?	When will our world end?
Will time travel ever happen?	Do your friends and family love and care about you as much as you do them? Or more?
Will I be a world traveler?	
Will I make a big difference in the world?	What would the world be like without language? music? medicine?
Will I be a professional sports person?	
Will I ever be gay or bi?	What if I passed the love of my life on the street and didn't even know it?
What will it be like the first time? What age?	
What do I live for?	Why do the students in schools divide themselves into groups of popular and non-popular?
Will I end up an old hag?	
Will I end up like my parents/grandparents?	Why do there have to be deaths because people are gay or different?
How did I get here?	
How did the world get here?	Why are there drunk drivers on the streets? No one's doing anything about it.
What will my future hold concerning marriage and children?	Why can't people be accepted for who they are and not what they want to be?

The World Questions from Soundings I

Will there ever be world peace?	Where are they occurring?
Why do we have wars?	Why are they occurring?
Will there be a World War III?	When will there be peace in the Middle East? Who is involved?
How will the wars affect us?	
How will technology affect battles in the future?	How will "power-hungry" people affect the world?
What are current conflicts? How can they be resolved?	When will terrorism in Israel stop?
	How can we prevent terrorism?

continued

Is terrorism becoming a larger problem than before? Why?

Why do people commit terrorist acts?

Why do we kill people just because they are different?

Why do we use materials that cannot be recycled?

Why do we cut down trees and fail to replace them?

Will we ever deplete our natural resources?

Will the greenhouse effect kill us?

How many rainforests are cut down per year?

Will recycling affect the ozone layer?

Will hunger become an even bigger problem?

Is there a lot of famine in the world?

What will we do when the air is unbreathable?

Will rainforests be replenished or destroyed?

Are we ever going to run out of food?

Are we going to bury ourselves beneath our own trash?

Is the government covering up info on aliens?

Will Clinton be impeached?

Will the stock market go "boom"?

How will the euro affect Europe?

Will the value of money ever drop?

What will happen with the world economic crisis?

Will we be the cause of the end of the world?

Will people ever become extinct?

What caused the beginning of the world?

How did the universe begin?

How will technology affect the world?

How will technology change the future?

How will it be available for us to use?

Will technology take over our jobs and future lives?

Will computers crash in 2000?

Will technology ever overpower manual labor?

How will cloning affect our lives?

Will they ever come out with an electric car?

Are we ever going to find a new source of power?

Will all the computers crash in the year 2000?

How fast can news be spread in the future?

Will TV ever be 3D?

Will television be advanced to a new level?

What problems may occur in the year 2000?

Will there ever be electric cars on the road?

Will a modern technology wave take over our schools?

Where do diseases originate?

Will there be cures for deadly diseases?

Will there ever be a way to prevent birth defects?

Will the death rate increase or decrease in the future?

Will we find life on other planets?

Are aliens really out there?

Will we travel to other planets?

Will people ever go live on other planets? If so, how will we be able to breathe?

Will people reach the earth's core?

How does space exploration affect us?

Will we find new species of land and water animals?

Will any new religions be created?

Will there be many more gangs?

Will there be any more cult suicides?

Why do the people in cults get sucked in?

How does immigration affect our country?

Is immigration going to be a worldwide problem?

Will there be another crisis like the Holocaust?

How many deaths a year result from drugs?

continued

How many teens a year get pregnant? Does this increase birthrates?

How does abortion affect our world?

How does population affect our world?

Why is there racism?

Will people ever be treated equally for who they are?

How fast has technology grown in the last 10 years? Will it ever take over humans?

Will the sun ever go out?

If we lose all our rainforests, is it possible we can die?

How do leader scandals affect the country?

How many abortions are done a year? Does this increase death and life rates?

Will racism problems worsen?

How many child laborers are working? Can or have any of them died, because of the labor?

How many die a year from abuse?

What is the punishment for child and/or adult abuse?

How many rapes occur a year?

What will be the result of the issues in Kosovo?

Will any new species be discovered? If so, will they help medicine?

Will cloning expand to human life?

Will limbs or organs be cloned for transplants? How?

Will cars ever be made solar or mechanic?

Will solar power ever take over electricity?

Will men ever be able to carry children?

Will there be a woman leader, president, empress?

Will space exploration advance?

Will people ever be able to travel past Pluto?

Will alcohol and drugs ever be banned?

Will life spans increase? How much?

Will the oceans ever dry up in a very serious drought?

Are there home run hitters like McGwire and Sosa in foreign countries?

Will there ever be a war about clashing religions or cultural beliefs?

Will any new building materials be made to cut down pollution?

Will there ever be a time when no one smokes? Or drinks?

Will education advance with technology, as in new computers-Internet classes?

Will teen pregnancy no longer be a problem in the future because more teens are becoming pregnant; so it is now semi-normal?

Are the beliefs that the cults have a disease of their mind, or just from pressure from others in the cult?

Why can't we arrange peace treaties instead of bombing/killing each other?

Will new diseases be created by man-made environments?

Will there ever be faster and more advanced medicine?

When will a cure for diseases such as AIDS or cancer be discovered?

Will we find information about the past from exploring in the future?

What are the most common diseases that are deadly, and how many people do they kill each year?

What has been the biggest act of terrorism in the nearest history?

What impact does the ozone layer have on us and on the environment?

Of the largest cities in the U.S., which have the most pollution, and where does it come from?

Will pollution ever worsen to the point that the earth is uninhabitable? How?

continued

Why can't we help kids with mental issues like kids with guns?	How does child labor in other countries affect U.S. children?
Are school shootings going to become worse?	How will the economic crisis affect us and our families?
Have school shootings occured outside of the United States? Why?	Will there ever be enough economy that will wipe out poverty and homelessness?
Will there be enough job opportunities for everyone?	What is going on in Asia involving the economy?
Will the falling Russian economy affect the U.S. stock market?	

One concern that is frequently voiced to me by educators is that middle level students will not ask serious or significant questions; they will be silly and suggest trivial questions designed for fun rather than rigorous study. My experience has shown this simply not to be the case. Once again, the reader will surely agree that the students came up with some truly excellent questions, ones adults in many walks of life deal with all the time. And these two lists are quite typical. In fact, each year's class comes up with remarkably similar lists of these questions, as do the many different groups of students and adults I've demonstrated this process with at conferences and meetings around the country. The bottom line is that young adolescents are grappling with complex issues; to assume they are only trivial thinkers does them a grave disservice.

Young adolescents are grappling with complex issues; to assume they are only trivial thinkers does them a grave disservice.

What's more, I have seen even apparently whimsical questions, such as "Is there really a Santa Claus?" lead groups into important discussions of cultural values, traditions, and belief systems. At a recent NMSA conference session where a number of us were demonstrating this process with 50 students from two local middle schools, one of the questions asked was "When is lunch?" Though suggested at first humorously, Barb Brodhagen focused on this question, asked for clarification, and soon the students were building a theme that included considerations of nutrition, traditions, time, and even poverty. ("What about people who never get to eat lunch?") Not only did Barb validate the student's question, she steered the conversation so students could uncover deeper meanings in their own questions. This showed them once again the interconnected nature of knowledge and reinforced the fundamental validity of their search for truth. No question need be seen as silly.

Another concern I frequently hear from educators touches on a central element of curriculum integration. Many teachers have said to me, "Since the students always ask the same types of questions, why not save time and just pre-plan a curriculum for them based on those questions?" While I can appreciate the apparent logic of the question, it actually misses a key and fundamental point of curriculum integration: namely, the empowerment of the students to own their curriculum. We have to remember that though I see the similar lists year after year, to the students, each year's list is uniquely theirs. That they will later see that they share many questions with the rest of humanity in no way diminishes the personal significance of the questions they themselves posed. To produce thinkers, rather than passive receptacles, we must honor the process.

At the same time, I recognize that teachers are faced with requirements and standards that are often overwhelming in number.

Aligning standards in a cohesive way to student-generated issues cuts down on the repetition that takes so much time and places so many extra burdens on students and teachers.

Part of what makes them overwhelming is the repetition of similar standards across different disciplines, each trying to account for much the same thing separately. I also hope that it is clear how easy it would be to attach many types of local standards to an examination of many of these important questions. Aligning standards in a cohesive way to these student-generated issues cuts down on the repetition that takes so much time and places so many extra burdens on students and teachers.

Consolidating questions and reaching consensus

The job of theme building is underway but far from complete. The students need to identify areas of overlap between the two sets of questions. One of the easiest ways to accomplish this is to have students walk around the room reviewing the lists and recording in notebooks those questions they think are represented on both lists. Again, representation can mean that the exact same question appears on each list, or it can mean that questions with similar content or direction appear. For example, we see on both lists the question: Will there be a World War III? Perhaps less immediately obvious, but just as significant, on the list of Self questions we see the concern: Why do the students in schools divide themselves into groups of popular and non-popular? On the World list there are similar questions about relationships on a larger scale, such as Why do we kill people just because they are different? and Will there ever be a war about clashing religions or cultural beliefs?

As students find similar or related questions, we color-code the connections on the existing sheets; or a new master list can be constructed on a large sheet of paper, on the board, or on a computer. We don't worry about seeing questions appear multiple times in different relationships; this just serves to enhance the process and demonstrate different avenues we can eventually follow to address the same questions.

In addition, identifying these similar or related questions helps the students see a direct link between their own individual concerns and issues facing the world at large. This linkage is vital to the sense of ownership we are building. Furthermore, it will eventually allow us to tackle more readily any content that the district says we have to cover because we will have established a student-generated context for that content. This virtually eliminates the question "Why do we have to learn this?" so often encountered in traditional curricula. Now the students have built their own connections and can use them effectively to learn any required information. So we start to group these common questions into categories or umbrella questions that can subsume many of the others. Wiggins and McTighe (1999), in their work on understanding by design, or backward planning, would call these the essential questions, the larger issues we want students to hold on to when they leave us.

There are several strategies we can use to identify the umbrella questions. One enjoyable way to do this is to give each student about eight colored self-stick dots and print his or her name neatly on each dot. Then the students stroll around the room and place their dots next to the questions they think are the most important. I often encourage them to do this without talking, just to help them focus on their own choices and not be swayed by someone else's arguments, comments, or pleas; but I have also done it while allowing talking, and that works well, too.

Patterns of preference quickly begin to emerge. Discussion of these preferences and the links established previously help narrow the dozens of questions down to a more manageable number. Because there is no one right way to interconnect questions, there cannot be just one correct or exclusive set of umbrella questions. Because the connections are made by the class through discussions in which one idea triggers another that refines another that leads to yet another, it is impossible in retrospect to reconstruct the pathways that brought us to a particular set of broad questions. Each year's class starts off with very similar questions from the initial steps of the process, but each has gone off in very different directions at this categorizing stage. For example, from the first year's two lengthy lists, we eventually generated a number of umbrella questions such as the following:

- Who am I and how did I get to be this way?
- What does the future hold for me, and what will influence my future?
- How did the universe and everything come to be?
- What is happening to the universe and the earth, and how does it affect me?
- What are emotions and what impact do they have on me?
- What is technology and how does it affect my life?
- How does culture affect people?

Considerable discussion in table groups and then with the whole class leads to identifying broad questions and ultimately themes.

These broad questions became our hooks for various possible themes. Table groups each took one question, returned to the original lists, and identified every original question that they thought fit under their respective umbrella. This gave us the opportunity to see which umbrella questions might provide the most bang for our buck, so to speak. The process also enabled the class to refine its understanding of what each larger question could entail.

Then the students began to have some fun with naming possible themes based on these groups of questions. That year's group came up with six they liked the most: The Twilight Zone, Technology, Lifestyles, Emotions, All About Me, The Future. The reader will undoubtedly be able to trace the origin of all of these, with the possible exception of The Twilight Zone. That name came up as students thought about questions of the past, the present, and the future, which led them to dimensions, which then reminded them of the old Rod Serling television series and its 1983 movie remake of that name.

The issue of naming themes can be problematic. One school of thought suggests that the overarching question ought to become the theme's title. This, proponents argue, prevents the theme from being seen as trivial and keeps the focus squarely on the essential questions involved. That is certainly a point well taken. Another school of thought suggests that allowing students to determine catchy, even idiosyncratic titles for themes enhances their sense of ownership—also a point well taken. I have tried it both ways over the years, and, frankly, I see little difference as long as the essential questions are clearly spelled out. So we often end up with unique titles followed by subtitles detailing the major question. For example, one year the students titled a theme "Exploring Above and Below Us: How are space and oceanic exploration similar and different?"

In the case of the first Soundings class, whose progress we have been following in greater detail, their discussions led to a number of consensus building compromises that resulted in "The Twilight Zone" being selected as the title for their entire year with subtitles for the three major themes that they linked together. Which brings us to a logistical consideration: how many themes do we attempt to design and implement each year? My rule of thumb is a maximum of three, and I explain this to the students early in the theme building process. They are quick to realize the reasoning behind this; namely, that to try to build and follow through with more than three themes would mean too little time could be devoted to some or all of the themes, depending on how the time was distributed.

Ideally, as was the case in year one, the students will find ways to connect themes. The Twilight Zone eventually encompassed *The Big Bang: How Did the Universe, Humans, and Cultures Begin? Technology: How Has Technology Changed History?* and *The Future: What Might My Life Be Like?* In Chapter 6 we will see how students constructed a framework for their year.

A fundamental point of curriculum integration is empowering students to own their currciulum.

CHAPTER SIX

Turning a Theme Concept
Into a Real Study

*Although I have only been in SOUNDINGS for two months,
I can already feel my self-confidence increasing. The deep
discussions and issues being brought up in class are so much more
advanced and intriguing that I feel I must share my thoughts.*
—Stephanie C.

Having determined the themes for the year, the time has come to begin shaping those themes into actual units of study. The first part of this task has already been started as we assembled the sub-questions that will be included in each theme. Next, we need to make sure we have not missed any important questions. Having selected the focus for each theme, we take a few minutes to consider that focus and give students a chance to ask any additional questions they may have specifically about the chosen topic. This step always generates important points that help refine and direct the eventual unit of study.

Now we need to put all the questions into some sort of priority that will enable us to devise a structure for the unit. One method for doing this is to have the class rank the questions in order of importance to them. Another is to look for a logical pattern to the questions; perhaps a chronological approach makes the most sense, or maybe a cause and effect relationship exists among the questions. Students never cease to amaze me with their insights and ideas at this organizing point. I usually have little to do other than to facilitate the discussion and make sure every voice gets heard.

I am likely to throw into the mix a couple of additional important considerations. I ask the students quite specifically to address the question, "What skills and background knowledge will we need to answer our questions?" This allows the group to generate a list of skills and background knowledge they think will be needed. Regardless of the theme topic, the initial list always includes items any teacher or administrator would want to see: research skills, reading skills, writing skills, listening skills, note-taking skills, organizational and time management skills. Often these are further delineated into more specific Internet search skills such as assessing Internet site validity, narrowing search queries, broadening search queries, and recording sources properly.

The initial list of skills is posted prominently in the room because we will be adding to it as we go through the next steps of the planning process. Eventually, other specific skills will be added depending on the precise nature of the unit plan. For example, we might need to add interviewing skills, map skills, presentation skills, drawing skills, video or photography skills, debate skills, or outlining skills. The crucial point here is that the students identify the skills that are essential to them in their quest to answer their questions. So, if we find a need to introduce a particular writing skill—let's say using commas after introductory dependent clauses—the students see the mini-lesson in the context of their need to write effectively about their research.

Students identify the skills that are essential to them in the quest to answer their questions.

Another related question I raise concerns state and local standards. I am not concerned about the most important standards, which tend to be the process standards. As the reader can readily see from the lists of skills the students decide they need, such process standards can be easily met and, I would argue, more willingly accepted by the students who can view them in the context of their own goals. I refer here instead to the more content specific subject area goals. Perhaps our district says we have to cover the American Revolution or ancient Mesopotamia or the periodic table of elements or even a particular novel or play. Now is the time to put these requirements in front of the students, to ask them, "What does the world expect us to know?" Then we let them figure out how best to work any such requirements into their themes. If we're looking at a theme such as "Why Can't People Get Along?" for example, we could easily use the American Revolution or even ancient Mesopotamian conflicts as a focus example. Clearly any number of required novels could also fit such a theme, since almost all literature involves conflict of one sort or another.

We could even use the periodic table of elements to illustrate how certain groups of chemicals form family-like bonds but don't mix well with certain other chemicals.

Empowering students to make such connections is at the very heart of all learning, and in particular of curriculum integration. Students are encouraged to use higher-level thinking skills to analyze and synthesize concepts and then draw conclusions. They are asked to construct their own sense of reality, to find and make meaning, and not merely to accept someone else's ideas of meaning. This is at once the essence of learning and the essence of democracy: honoring and entrusting each individual to determine his or her own sense of the world, and doing so in the context of a positive shared vision with others. Thus we serve our students better and still address local standards by using curriculum integration to link society's predetermined standards and requirements with the students' personal concerns. The message once again is in the medium, in the very process of curriculum integration; and the rhetoric becomes reality through practice.

> *Empowering students to make such connections is at the very heart of all learning, and in particular of curriculum integration.*

At least three other vital considerations must be purposefully addressed in this theme planning process. Having given our questions some degree of priority, having listed some of the skills we will need to answer our questions, and having explored ways to tie our questions to local standards, we now ask ourselves, "What resources do we have available to help us answer our questions?"

As has been the case many times in this process, such a question may be addressed in the middle of the class discussion or handed over to table groups to discuss and then share results with the class. The query can just as easily be raised as a log question the day before we will devote class discussion time to this issue. I have introduced the issue both ways with equal success. Invariably, students will list the Internet, the library/media center, and the books in the classroom as the more obvious resources. It doesn't take long, however, for students to go beyond the obvious and suggest interviews (by phone, e-mail, or regular mail) with parents, relatives, local experts, and nowadays even far distant experts. Polling and surveying for opinions often come up. Guest speakers, field trips, movies and videos all emerge as potential sources of information. In many cases, designing and conducting firsthand experiments is also an appropriate and feasible method for obtaining data.

Again, putting the onus on the students empowers them and excites them to go beyond the normal classroom resources and explore their topic questions in the world at large. At the same time, many of these resources require certain skills to be used most effectively; so those skills can be added to our list and will help us meet many local standards.

With all these elements worked into our thinking, it is time to look toward end results. At this point, we ask the students to think about how they would like to show the world what they have learned and accomplished. Through our usual three-step procedure, individuals, small groups, and then the class as a whole, we build a list of potential products or outcomes. Often this will include essays, research papers (remember the students agreed to do two of these when they elected to be in the program), museum or fair-like presentations, posters, murals, models, videos, plays, short stories, poems, dances, musical works, oral reports, and any number of apropos community service projects.

We then look over this list of possible products and compare it with our lists of questions, skills, local requirements, and resources. The students also discuss their personal preferences and learning styles: some like to perform, others prefer to write or to build something. Consequently, with an eye always toward compromise and consensus, the class usually comes up with a combination of several of these.

Examples of sharing activities

The varied activities carried out by the more recent Soundings VI provide good examples of the creative ways students devise to share what they have learned. Before returning to the story of how Soundings I developed its first unit, these examples will illustrate not only the ways students in this program carry out their commitment to share what they have learned but also the extent and depth of their research. This class had planned a unit to explore questions about ways life in cultures from different times and places were similar and different. Their unit questions included:

- What is culture, and how does it affect us?
- What makes life so different in different cultures?
- How has time affected different cultures?
- How do different cultures influence each other?
- How is entertainment different in different cultures?

- How does religion influence art?
- What are some art forms from different cultures?
- What kinds of foods do people in different cultures eat, and what can that tell us about their cultures?
- What kinds of houses do people live in, and what does that tell us about them?
- How and why has language changed?
- Does the religion of a culture affect its government?
- What do people's clothing reveal to us about their beliefs?

Given the range of these questions (and there were many more included in the sub-question list) and the fact that certain students were keenly interested in particular cultures (medieval European cultures were popular, as were Asian cultures), the class elected to involve themselves in a series of six major projects. Furthermore, after listing a large number of possible cultures representing the entire planet and span of cultural existence, the students decided to focus on seven examples. They chose the Second Kingdom of Ancient Egypt, Rome around the time of Christ, the Viking culture of the 9th century, English culture around the time of the Norman Conquest, French culture in the 12th and 13th centuries, Japanese culture in the 13th century, and contemporary Chinese culture. Students picked the culture in which they had the most interest; research and presentation groups formed accordingly.

In addition, they chose to take this opportunity to complete their first major research paper. The research paper, requirements for which can be found in Appendix 2, allowed students to select areas and questions of particular personal issue that we might not be able to address comprehensively as a class. Thus one student worked on medieval sieges while another researched the history of Japanese samurai. One student studied the Pol Pot/Khmer Rouge regime and its effects on Cambodia, while another explored Zen influences on Japanese gardens and architecture. I'll have more to say on research paper projects later. For now, suffice it to say that these individual projects are a great way to demonstrate mastery of many different skills while empowering students to pursue personal interests.

Individual projects are a great way to demonstrate mastery of many different skills while empowering students to pursue personal interests.

The remaining six projects accounted for the small group and whole class aspects of the unit. The students decided to hold feast days to share what they learned about food, fashion shows to describe clothing, and game days to teach each other sports and games enjoyed in their respective cultures. They also decided to share answers to questions about languages through either a video production or a board game. Each group would also contribute exhibits of visual arts to a cultural art museum, and thus address the many questions about the arts and culture.

The culminating piece, however, was to be a scale model of a town or village from their culture. These models, along with photos and artifacts from the other five presentations, were to be displayed for the entire school and parents to see.

Deciding on these results was just the first piece of this stage. For each mini-project, the students next made a list of criteria. They asked, What would a good Feast Day include? or What would a good fashion show look like? or What would each involve? This is where the creativity, the ingenuity, and, indeed, the beauty of the process begin to shine.

For the feast day, the class decided that each group would prepare and serve at least two samples of foods common to their chosen culture. The "meal," however, would start with a menu. This menu would describe many common foods, just as one might find in a real restaurant. On the back of the menu, the students would present information about the foods. They could describe who ate which foods, if there were social restrictions; or they could illustrate the symbolism attached to various foods. They could describe special preparation or serving techniques. In addition, the group would provide copies of the recipes used to prepare the sample

The Medieval Banquet was one of seven held as each group provided food samples and more that were representative of the culture studied.

foods. Not only did this help give a clearer picture of the culture's foods, it also helped avoid any problems with food allergies. Students with any such allergies—and we had a few in the class—could read the recipe and elect not to partake of any sample that might contain something harmful to them.

We had seven most interesting meals a few weeks later. My favorite, I must admit, was the French banquet. The group rearranged all the tables in our room to form a large U-shape, and covered the tables with linen tablecloths. On the head table they placed a large salt bowl, and my teaching partner and I were given the only two seats at this table as "king and queen" for the feast. The other students were assigned social rankings and seated accordingly, with the highest-ranking nobles nearest the salt and the lower vassals at the far ends. The group then served us from large platters. We ate with our hands while a juggler—admirably played by one young lady from the group—entertained us all.

The fashion show also went beyond the run-of-the-mill presentation one often sees in social studies classes. The students decided to use the auditorium, making the center aisle the runway, which led to the chorus risers at the foot of the stage. Models wearing clothing typical of the respective cultures would sashay down the aisle, up the risers, then back and forth across the proscenium. Meanwhile a narrator with a microphone described the fashions in full detail, just as one would expect to hear in the great fashion salons of New York or Paris.

A genuine fashion show complete with runway and narrator was presented in the auditorium by those who had done extensive study of these seven cultures.

Fox and Geese, a Viking board game.

Asianopoly.

Old Norse Language Game.

In addition, the groups had to produce several pages of drawings and descriptions of the same clothes. These pages served as a guide or brochure for the fashion show, and they presented much of the pertinent information in response to specific questions about the role of clothing in a culture. The brochures also went on display for our final celebration, along with pictures, including the ones you see here.

For sports and entertainment, the class decided to require each group to teach the class one physical sport and one game from the culture it chose. The goal was to involve everyone in at least one and preferably both activities. In many cases, the less physical game was played as the sport contestants were eliminated, thus keeping all occupied. The rules were to be printed up and distributed, along with a description of the game or sport's history, who played it, when and perhaps why they played it, and any other pertinent information. Several weeks later we enjoyed modified Sumo wrestling, an ancient version of soccer, and a wonderfully creative jousting match, along with several types of card games and board games from the different cultures.

For the language presentation, each group was to find out how the language of its chosen culture originated, changed over time, and influenced other languages. Results could be presented in a game format, or a video; but all were due on the same day. Each presentation was to last ten minutes, and the students would rotate through each other's activities while taking turns monitoring or presenting their own group's.

Displays of Chinese, Medieval English, and Medieval French art were included in the art musuem.

The art museum was handled in a similar manner. Each group had to research the popular and fine arts typical of its chosen culture. Then they had to produce at least two original works representative of those arts. These had to be made by students; they could not simply be copied from a book or the Internet; nor could they be commercially manufactured.

Most groups included posters describing the arts of their chosen culture. Most groups produced more than the requisite two examples. These works were displayed again in the final celebration.

The model village had the most criteria, as one would expect, since the students considered it the central part of their project. The class decided that all the models would be built on identical 4' x 4' wooden bases. Groups were encouraged to create an appropriate landscape on this base before constructing the village. Thus while the Egyptian landscape remained virtually flat, the Viking group created steep slopes descending to a fjord; and the French group made rolling hills.

The groups were then to incorporate the following places or facilities within their culture's villages:

- Where food was served: homes, taverns, communal dining hall
- Where food came from: farms, markets
- Houses for each social class in that culture
- Place(s) of worship, if there were any
- Place of government
- Place where entertainment occurred
- Place for education, be it at home, school, or religious institution
- Work places: e.g., forges, smiths, factories, farms
- Market, shops, or place for trading
- Protection facilities or structures
- Transportation facilities: paths, roads, harbors

- Burial/cremation sites
- Monuments
- Places and methods for waste disposal
- Other unique features special to the culture: wells, fountains, bath houses.

The Japanese village met all criteria set by students.

A one- or two-page descriptive summary of all these elements was to be displayed near the model. A map of the village's location was also to be included so visitors would be able to see quickly where this hypothetical village would have been. A background scene was deemed optional. Each group could determine its own scale based on the different size needs of the groups, but that scale had to be displayed as well.

In addition to deciding the elements that needed to be included, the class also discussed other characteristics that would help them determine success. Concepts like historical accuracy, maintaining appropriate scale, neatness, and completeness were brought up. So, too, were ideas such as equity and responsibility, proper and effective use of time and materials, and overall cooperative functioning of the group; all were added to our preparations for making the best projects we could.

... as did this Medieval French village, shown with its creators.

A final step taken before actually commencing the research and "doing" stages of the unit was to determine our time line. Looking at the calendar of the remaining months, we first selected a reasonable date for the final celebration when we would share all of this with the world. This always requires careful consideration and some degree of flexibility. In our case, it involved scheduling our use of the activities center, which is used by many groups, day and night, throughout the year. We also had to consider the eighth grade musical with its demanding rehearsal and performance schedule, as many Soundings students take part in this extravaganza each year. Sports schedules, holidays, and other types of events all enter into the picture and narrow our possibilities. A student volunteer creates a giant wall calendar, and we fill in all the pertinent dates. Finally, through a process of compromise and elimination, we schedule a firm date with the office, a solid deadline.

Then we work back from that date. We look at each part of the overall project and discuss how much time we think each will require to complete. The students look at ways to multitask and overlap. They search for ways to have one part of a project help complete another part. Bit by bit the calendar gets filled in with due dates for all the many parts of the unit. Students then type up the calendar on the computer. Copies get printed, distributed to students and parents, and posted around the room.

With the basic planning stage over, we are ready at last to begin working in earnest on our unit. Keep in mind, there will be ongoing debriefings, and we will tweak interim due dates as we get ahead of or fall behind schedule. The daily log questions and daily goal setting procedures will help keep us on track and constantly aware of where we are and where we need to be. Less time, however, will be spent on discussions now; far more time will be given over to the students to work independently or with their small groups. The room gets very busy, often a blur of activity and noise. I, for one, love it.

Before turning our attention back to Soundings I, I want to add an additional word about the planning process. Again, while the elements delineated are critical, the strategies one could use to get to them are numerous. I don't always use the same ones, and I certainly don't claim to have found the best way. Sometimes all of our discussions are with the entire class. Sometimes we form volunteer steering committees to take the general ideas from the class and flesh out a unit plan to bring back to the class for approval or amendment. Sometimes we do combinations and throw in one of those ranking votes I described earlier to speed up the process if needed. What really matters is the consistent level of empowerment that is maintained throughout the process. The teachers guide and facilitate but don't ever try to push the class in a predetermined direction. That would spell immediate disaster, as the students would sense hypocrisy and trust would be lost.

This is a difficult task. During her first year in Soundings, one of my teaching partners, when asked by a visitor what was the hardest part of coming into such a student-driven program, replied, "Keeping my mouth shut. I've had to bite the inside of my cheek a lot!" A teacher's natural proclivities are to talk. However, students learn more when they are talking and doing than when they are merely listening. Teachers need to talk less and listen more so students can talk more and listen less.

When teachers master the skill of keeping quiet, students recognize they truly are empowered. Then both students and teachers are liberated, free to go about the business of real learning in a democratic community.

It is not uncommon to have a guest actively working with students on a special project.

CHAPTER SEVEN

Our Community of Learners Pursues "The Twilight Zone"

When you get to pick what you are going to study, it
makes studying that topic a lot more fun.

—Chris M.

I submit for your edification, 40 young adolescents. By their own choice, they find themselves outside the conventional curriculum, thrust into a nebulous region without a preset plan or course of study, surrounded by hundreds of unanswered questions, bolstered only by a still-being-formed vision of a democratic classroom. Can they survive? Can they prevail? Can they excel?

Welcome to the Twilight Zone.

As we noted previously, this theme in Soundings I eventually encompassed three major sub-themes or strands. Using the same process described in the last chapter, the students decided that *The Big Bang: How Did the Universe, Humans, and Cultures Begin?* would be their first unit. *Technology: How Has Technology Changed History?* would take up the bulk of the spring as a second unit, and *The Future: What Might My Life Be Like?* would be a shorter, final unit. Again, as we saw in the previous chapter, the estimated time divisions were based on the questions to be pursued in each unit and the kinds of final products the class wanted to prepare and present to the world. Come with me as we go through each unit and see in detail how the students implemented the process and their plans.

UNIT ONE: THE BIG BANG

While reviewing initial questions and supplementing them with additional ones, the students determined that there was a pattern among the questions. While they all had to do with beginnings or how things started, the questions fell into categories. One category was the physical universe, including the solar system, galaxies, and other astronomical phenomena. A second category concerned human evolution, while a third addressed issues pertaining to the rise of cultures. The unit questions are listed below.

Unit Questions

How did the universe begin?
- How was the universe created?
- What are the major theories?
- Who proposed these theories?
- How do theories vary by culture?
- How do we test theories?

How does the universe function?
- What is the universe?
- What is it made of?
- How big is the universe?
- How old is the universe?
- What "laws" appear to control it?
- Is there a space-time continuum?
- Is space curved?
- When will the universe end?
- How does our solar system operate?
- What are the planets like?
- How do the planets and the sun interact with each other?
- How does gravity work?

How was the earth created?
- What are the major theories?
- Who proposed these theories?
- How do theories vary by culture?
- How do we test theories?
- How old is the earth?
- What is the earth made of?

- What is the earth's structure?
- What is the earth's magnetic field?
- What does it look like?
- How does it operate?
- How does it help us?
- Has it ever changed?
- What theories explain our moon?
- What is the moon made of?
- How does our moon relate to others?
- How does the moon relate to the earth?

How have land forms changed?
- What was the original land form structure?
- What arrangements has the land had in the past?
- What caused the changes?
- What are plate tectonics?
- Why do volcanoes occur?
- How do volcanoes work?

How did humans evolve?
- What is the theory of evolution?
- What is involved in the theory of evolution?
- Who first proposed this theory? When?
- How do scientists test the theory?
- Why do organisms evolve?

continued

How did humans evolve?

- Does evolution require a certain kind of environment?
- How do stages of evolution differ?
- How long does it take to complete a stage of evolution?
- How do animals live in different environments?
- How did life get so diverse?
- Do animals continue to evolve?
- What happened to the dinosaurs?
- Are there any creatures living today in the same form/stage as long ago?
- If so, why haven't they changed?
- Did humans evolve from other life forms?
- What were the first life forms?
- Which other life forms came before humans?
- When and where did the first humans appear?
- How have humans changed over time?
- How can we tell that we have changed?
- How did early humans communicate?
- How have different cultures explained the creation of humans?

How did cultures evolve?

- What is a culture?
- How do we define a culture?
- What elements do all cultures have in common?

How and where did cultures form?

How do cultures represented by
- subsistence culture: Native American
- agricultural culture: Middle Ages
- early industrial culture: Colonial America
- fully industrialized culture

compare/contrast with respect to:
- family structures
- marriage conventions
- medical treatment
- education
- government
- art
- agriculture
- recreation/sport

What caused any differences in the areas listed?

In light of these categories, the students decided to divide themselves into groups according to personal interest. Those most interested in the physical universe would take charge of those questions, for example, while other groups formed to attack the remaining set of questions. We agreed, however, that it was vital for everyone eventually to become knowledgeable about all the information, so the students formulated a plan to ensure that this would happen.

First, members of each group divided up their set of questions, researched answers, and prepared a summary response to each question. These would then be collected into a Big Bang Book that would ultimately be photocopied for everyone in the class. Each student would present his or her questions and answers orally to the class as well in order to make sure everyone understood the information and had a chance to ask for clarification. Going along with this summary and presentation, each student was to put together a poster display or three-dimensional model illustrating some aspect of the answers found.

This would constitute their first major research project and prepare them to do a full research paper in the second unit. Consequently, we asked them to take advantage of all the research resources they had listed and to keep a record of all those sources.

Resources included interviewing experts, so we encouraged students to ask local experts they encountered to be guest speakers for the class. We called this Adopt-a-Guest, based on a similar strategy I had used for years in the Watershed program. Students would find an authority in the field being studied and invite that person to speak to the class. The student would provide the speaker with helpful background information about Soundings and our theme and then make arrangements with the speaker for a convenient date and time. On the day of the speaker's visit, the student host would greet the guest upon arrival, introduce the speaker to the class, assist the guest during the talk if needed, thank the guest at the end of the talk, and finally escort him or her back to the office to sign out. One last responsibility involved sending a follow-up thank-you note to the guest. Not only did this result in a large number of excellent guest speakers throughout the year, it also enhanced students' growing self-confidence and maturity as they fulfilled all the responsibilities.

My teaching partner and I were charged with responsibilities, too. We were asked to provide introductory lessons and information for all three theme areas so the entire class would have the same basic foundation knowledge and a common vocabulary when it came time for all the different presentations. We had access to films and videos that would be beneficial for the class to see. We used the log questions as an avenue to introduce key concepts. We put together an activity packet on basic principles and definitions from physics and chemistry that students would need to understand as they looked for answers to their questions. This packet included concepts such as matter, energy, velocity, acceleration, and gravity, among a number of others. Articles we pulled from numerous sources provided daily opportunities for shared oral reading and class discussions. We even did a clam dissection lab, similar to what was being done in the regular science classes; but we tied ours to understanding physiology and taxonomy in relation to evolution.

The class, in early unit discussions, decided that the final celebration or presentation of all of this learning would be a Big Bang Museum. This museum, to be held over a two-day period in the activities center, would be a chance to display individual projects and share the results of their research. As work progressed, students refined this idea in a couple of interesting ways. First, they had already determined that they wanted to invite the entire school to see their projects, and they also wanted to invite their parents to tour the museum. The students had met many local experts who gave them valuable assistance in their search for answers. They wanted to share their work with these people, so the invitation list grew significantly.

The class further decided that they needed a way to set up the museum that would be more interesting and more like a real museum than typical school project displays. The solution: design a set of panels that would be used as freestanding dividers to designate the focus areas of the museum. Each research group would get three

Student examines a skull in preparing for its display in the museum.

4' x 8' panels hinged together so they could stand as a grouping without additional support. The research team would design a mural and paint it on the panels. This mural would be an artistic way to convey even more information about their topic. As the panels were freestanding, the mural would have to cover both sides, effectively creating a mural that would be 24 feet long and 8 feet tall. We like to dream *big*!

As if that weren't big enough, the students decided that when the museum was over, we should put all nine panels together to make one truly huge, two-sided mural. This meant that the designers had to be cognizant of each other's pieces of the mural so they could all somehow look cohesive when put together. So, as they worked, they shared ideas and coordinated plans among the three groups.

But wait; there's more! In the course of their initial research, a few students in two of the original groups—cultures and the universe—began to see that they were actually dealing with the same issue: namely, how different cultures have explained the beginnings of the world. This small group asked to become a fourth group to present creation accounts from different cultures and different religions. It made sense to the class, so this new group formed. Of course, they would now need their own section in the museum, and that meant they needed their own set of panels, too. Because they were a smaller group, however, and because they were starting late on the mural design, they elected to use just two panels instead of three. Nevertheless, this raised the mural's total to 11 panels, some 88 feet of overall length.

And so work proceeded. Each day would begin with a reading of the class log. This, again, provided a ritual grounding for the community by reminding us all what we had accomplished the day before and, by extended discussion, what needed to be accomplished that day. The class log would be followed by a discussion of the quotation or the log question from the previous day. The log questions became much more content oriented once the unit began.

The log question discussion, including a reading of the next, newly posted log question, usually led us to a shared reading on a related topic. Some days, for example, we worked through the physics or chemistry packets. Other days we read articles together that my teaching partner and I had found and photocopied for the class. Occasionally we would read a related piece of literature, too. For example, while discussing cultural views of evolution, we read William Blake's poem, *The Tyger* and discussed it both as a work of art and as an artifact relating to views on evolution. Such literary readings and discussions allowed us to work with literary terms and concepts, thus meeting the standards of the language arts department in that respect; but more importantly, they allowed us to reinforce the real-world role of literature as very human commentary on the authors' worlds. This provides the students with a tangible context for works of literature, which, in turn, makes those works more accessible, meaningful, and thus memorable.

Following this, we would often break for a short cooperative challenge or game. That first year our room gave us direct access through a back stairway to the rarely used lower gym. Because physical education classes generally used this gym only in the winter, it was a great space for games like Snake in the Grass, Buttball, and Cookie Factory.

Returning to the room, we would take a few minutes to debrief the game. Then we would establish priorities for the remainder of the day. Often this meant asking groups to structure their work time and make sure each person in the group knew what needed to get done.

Occasionally we scheduled library or computer room time so students could work on their research. That first year we had only two computers in the room—now we have 20—so the library and the computer rooms were necessary adjuncts to our classroom. Now and again we would have a film or video to show during part of our day, and on some days we would have a guest speaker.

Sometimes we would have visitors who came to see how curriculum integration works in a real classroom. This continues to happen—indeed, with increasing regularity. Soundings VI had visitors in the room roughly 60 days of their year. Soundings I had far fewer such visits, probably more like 10 or 15 over the year, but whenever we have visitors, we take time to let them ask questions and have an open discussion with the students. Visitors are regularly amazed at the way Soundings students can articulate what they are doing and, more importantly, why they are doing what they do. I've even had visitors remark that Soundings must be a class of only "gifted" students. Though I personally believe every child is indeed gifted in some way, the term used in these instances is meant to indicate only students who had been identified through a test as having a certain IQ. By now the reader knows that Soundings is, in fact, heterogeneously grouped and includes students of all academic abilities.

At any rate, other than for activities such as these, the time then belonged to the students. They set about planning and preparing presentations, writing up their summary reports, putting together display materials, and of course, designing and painting the huge mural panels. We purchased 11 sheets of pressboard, a material similar to plywood, but made of wood chips and a bonding agent formed into 3/8" thick sheets by exposure to heat and high pressure. Readily available at any home improvement store or lumberyard, these sheets tend

Students designed and painted the huge mural panels that depicted what each group had gleaned from its research.

to be a little less expensive than plywood. To one side of these sheets, the students glued and nailed 1" x 2" boards to act as a framing that thickened the edges and gave the panels added rigidity. These frames also made it easier to attach the 3" door hinges we eventually used to connect the panels.

We had panels everywhere for several weeks.

Long before they were put together, however, the panels had to be primed. Then our best artists got to work transferring to the panels the mural designs, which had first been drawn on paper for the class's approval. We had panels everywhere for several weeks. Our room that year had a dropped ceiling that was only seven feet above the floor. Yes, it was a rather claustrophobic room in that sense, and it even had a three-foot-square column (one of the building's main support columns) running right up the center of the room. These two structural issues gave us fits all year as we struggled quite literally to work under and around them. For the mural panels, this meant moving tables to lay panels on the floor, removing ceiling tiles to stand the panels upright, and standing panels in the hallway outside our room.

Since this hallway also led to the cafeteria, it did ensure a high degree of visibility for our students as all the other students in the school passed by each day and could see the work in progress. This actually had very positive effects and generated a lot of interest in both the particular project and the program as a whole. Many students who signed up for Soundings II attributed their initial interest to seeing Soundings I students enjoying this work in the hallway.

Tangentially, we saw the reverse of this phenomenon the following year when we were assigned a room in the basement of our administration building next door to and across the bus driveway from the middle school building. Though some other students came to the administration building for world language classes, they did not have to pass the Soundings room, which was located at the farthest end of the floor. As a result, other students never witnessed what our students were doing that second year. In fact, they almost forgot we existed; and this, along with some staffing disruptions, caused us some small problems with getting interested students in the program the year after that.

Fortunately, we managed to survive despite such unfortunate logistical problems, and we moved to yet another room for years three and four. We moved again for years five, six, seven, and now eight. Next year Soundings IX will move into the new middle school that Soundings VI students had a small hand in designing. This new building has rooms especially designed for our three integrated programs, so we should have fewer space and location related problems.

Returning to year one's efforts, as research progressed, work days eventually involved individual reports and group presentations in addition to the other activities previously described. We took time out for a literary coffeehouse or two, and, of course, we continued to break for cooperative games and challenges.

In the week right after the winter holiday, we sent out this invitation to the rest of the school.

Soundings

An Integrative Program for Eighth Graders

January 7, 1999

To: 5th, 6th, and 7th grade teams:

To give you as much lead-time as possible to help you in your planning, we would like to inform you of a special sequence of events involving the Soundings students later in January.

On Wednesday and Thursday, January 27 and 28, the Soundings students plan to present the results of their studies thus far. This presentation will take the form of a museum set up in the Activities Center. The museum will include numerous displays created by the students, along with their large (8-feet tall x 88-feet long!) mural depicting aspects of their research into the creation of the universe, the evolution of humans, and the development of culture.

On the afternoon of January 28th, the students will host a special showing of their work to their parents, Radnor administrators, and some very special invited guests including, among others, some professors from Haverford College, Bryn Mawr College, and the University of Pennsylvania. These guests will also interview the students as part of the assessment process.

---

continued

In addition to this special showing, we would like to invite your classes to visit the museum on Thursday morning between 8:15 and noon. Soundings students will be providing informative, guided tours to any interested 5th, 6th, and 7th grade classes. If members of your team would be interested in visiting the museum, please return the attached form to us as soon as possible so we can work out a schedule to avoid overcrowding.

We also hope you'll drop by the museum on Wednesday afternoon (as we practice) or anytime Thursday if you have a preparation period. The students would be pleased to share their efforts with you.

If you have any questions, please contact one of us. Thank you in advance for helping the students make this project successful.

Along with this invitation, we sent the following scheduling form:

Team : _____ Contact Person: _____

We would like to bring some/all (circle one) of our team's classes to the Soundings museum on Thursday, January 28th.

Please indicate your preference:

_____ We would like to bring the entire team at one time:
  _____ 8:15–9
  _____ 9–9:45
  _____ 9:45–10:30
  _____ 10:30–11:15
  _____ 11:15–12:00

_____ The following teachers would like to bring individual classes at these times:

Teacher's Name
  _____ 8:15–9
  _____ 9–9:45
  _____ 9:45–10:30
  _____ 10:30–11:15
  _____ 11:15–12:00

We will create a schedule and confirm times with you by January 20th.

To parents and others who had helped us, we sent the following letter on Soundings stationery:

January 7, 1999

Dear _____

On Wednesday and Thursday, January 27 and 28, the Soundings students plan to present the results of their studies thus far. This presentation will take the form of a museum set up in the Radnor Middle School's Activities Center. The museum will include numerous displays created by the students, along with their large (8 feet tall x 88 feet long!) mural depicting aspects of their research into the creation of the universe, the evolution of humans, and the development of culture. In addition to setting up this museum, the students will be providing informative tours to interested 5th, 6th, and 7th grade classes. Then, on the afternoon of January 28th, the students will host a special showing of their work to their parents, Radnor administrators, and some very special invited guests including, among others, some professors from Haverford College, Bryn Mawr College, and the University of Pennsylvania.

We would like to invite you to be part of this Thursday afternoon session. We plan to begin the presentations portion of the program at 12:30 p.m. This will be followed, starting around 1:15 p.m., with about 45 minutes of small roundtable discussions among adults and students. If we can get enough volunteers, we hope to have one or two adults meet with each group of about four students to ask questions and to give students a chance to show what they have learned about our topics. During these "informal" discussions, in addition to refreshments, we will provide the adults with a short assessment form to fill out on each student in their small group.

We hope you'll accept our invitation to be part of this important day. Please return the attached form to us as soon as possible to let us know whether or not you can be part of our discussion/assessment roundtables. If you cannot participate in the discussions, we still hope you will drop by the museum on Wednesday afternoon or anytime Thursday. The students would be pleased to share their efforts with you.

If you have any questions, please contact one of us. Thank you in advance for helping the students make this project successful.

Using the responses from these invitations, we planned our schedule of visitors for the two days of the museum showings. Preparations and rehearsals reached a fever pitch, and everything finally came together late in January as we moved the panels and all the project presentation materials to the activities center and set up our Big Bang Museum.

We hosted almost the entire school on those two days, with our students acting as tour guides, escorting groups through the museum and explaining the exhibits. Both students and teachers from the other teams were amazed at the scope and the depth of the investigations involved in answering the questions.

So, too, were the adult guests who attended the late afternoon session. Parents, our school district and building administrators, experts who had helped us, and other interested people arrived to see the museum. As they entered the activities center, each guest received a list of the essential questions to refer to for context as they toured the exhibits.

After an hour, we assembled our guests and asked them to spread themselves out at ten round tables we had set up. Each table had chairs for eight; so, with three or four adults at each table, we then asked the students to fill in the remaining four or five seats at each of the tables.

After the tour, guests and students assembled at round tables. The visitors were impressed, as the students were more than ready to discuss their work and the issues involved.

With everyone settled comfortably at a table, we asked the students and adults to introduce themselves to one another. Then the adults were asked to begin a question and answer discussion using their observations of the museum and any of the questions on the guide sheet. Adults could ask any of those questions of any student at the table. The only unacceptable answer would be something to the effect of, "That wasn't my area." We assumed that by now each student had had ample exposure to all the questions and would be able to give a meaningful response.

They admirably validated our assumption. Going from table to table, we were impressed with the level of discourse occurring, with most of it coming from the students. They were eager to show off their knowledge and understanding, and they reveled in the chance to discuss serious issues with adults, many of whom, though experts in one area, knew less about some of the other topics than the students did. The levels of student confidence and excitement grew perceptively over the hour that the discussions lasted.

When it was time to close, we asked the adults to give us some written feedback on the performance of the students at their table. As you can imagine, it was extremely positive.

When we debriefed the sessions with the students the next day, their overwhelming response was that they wished they had had more time to continue their discussions.

Did we need to give a paper and pencil test at this point to verify learning? Of course not. The students demonstrated their mastery of the information in an authentic, meaningful, and sophisticated way. They knew and openly remarked how thoroughly they felt they had learned the material. The process, starting with their own questions, followed by authentic research, which led to presenting their results in multiple ways (in writing, orally, and via the displays and murals), and finally articulating responses to their questions in discussions with adults, had helped them truly understand and internalize the information.

Senior citizens were among the many guests who attended the culminating event of our first unit.

UNIT TWO: TECHNOLOGY

Bolstered by their tremendous success, the students began planning to do even more in their second and longest unit of the year, Technology. From our initial work in September, we already had our essential questions, so we pulled those lists from the files, reviewed them, and added new questions. Our experience in the Big Bang unit made planning easier this time as the students now more fully appreciated the need for careful organization and time management. But they also appreciated how much more they could accomplish by using this curriculum integration process effectively.

The following questions were established for the technology unit.

Technology Questions

What is technology?

How has technology changed over time?
– What were some of the first technological advances?

How has changing technology affected the course of history?
– Has technology ever been the cause of wars?
– How has technology changed or influenced death rates in the past and present?

How has technology affected the way we live?
– What makes technology so important in our life?
– Why is technology changing the way we live?
– Why do people rely on technology so much?
– How does technology affect us personally?
– Is technology a danger to family life?
– Has technology divided people into classes?

How has technology affected
– the way we view our past and our future in our culture?
– human needs?
– medical treatment?
– sight?
– culture?
– entertainment?
– television?
– film production?
– performing arts?
– book production?
– music?
– photography?
– family life and activities?
– food?
– clothing?
– economics and prices of various items?
– marketing and stores?
– working people and businesses?
– the stock market?
– poverty?
– homelessness?
– industry?
– agriculture?
– the environment?

---

continued

- pollution?
- wildlife management?
- the ways we can help people?
- architects, designs, blueprints?
- building materials?
- famous people?
- safety and protection?
- criminal activities?
- the drug problem in America?
- crime prevention and law enforcement?

- lawyers?
- transportation?
- the military?
- politics?
- communications?
- mail?
- navigation?
- education?
- space exploration?
- scientific explorations?
- population?

What technological advances brought about vaccinations or treatments?

What new inventions have helped doctors?

How does information get transferred? How long does it take? What different forms?

How would education differ without technology?

How would childbirth and premature births differ without technology?

How is genetic engineering made possible by technology?

What has been done to help people without limbs?

How do microchips work?

How are newer buildings different from past ones?

How are atom bombs built?

How has media technology changed the physical appearance values of our culture?

Is the Internet better or worse than real stores for shopping?

What in technology influences teenaged girls to lose weight?

Has technology changed the relationship of the audience to the performing arts? All art?

Has technology changed the availability of different art forms?

Has technology changed the quality of performances?

Has technology changed the way people relate to each other and communicate?

With the Internet, will we still need books?

Once again, we see that these young adolescents had a lot of important questions on their minds! We also see that addressing all these questions would be impossible in a conventional class format. All that front-end loading really begins to pay off now as the students take charge. They looked at these questions, then looked at what the rest of the eighth grade was doing, and they came up with a remarkable, multifaceted plan. This plan combined several layers of individual and small group research, classroom activities, a novel, a play, use of the scientific method, writing, and community service into a cohesive unit. The final celebration for this unit was to be a "Big Bang-quet" late in May, but a lot of work would precede this celebratory feast.

The schematic diagram on p. 107 illustrates how tightly constructed this unit turned out to be. The unit started with the decision to focus the class's attention on the big questions and leave the more specific questions once again to individual and small group research. The students knew they had to write a research paper, so they easily decided that the topic for that paper should come from the list of very specific questions. Individuals would be free to select from that list a topic question that most interested them.

Yet, the students also liked the hands-on project approach as well. So they decided to combine the two. Once a student selected a research topic question, he or she would be responsible for a 3D mini-project presentation on some specific aspect of the question. For example, one young lady who hopes to become a doctor was particularly interested in questions about the effects technology has had on the practice of medicine. In her early research into this issue, she learned about discoveries that led to advances in patient treatment. She chose to do a diorama and mini-oral report on Harvey's experiments with the circulatory system. Another student, more attuned to the arts, wondered how technology changed the world of painting. This student discovered that the invention of the camera had a dramatic impact on painting, and made a model of an early camera, and told the class about its significance.

As we heard these presentations, we kept a time line in our notebooks to help us address one of our essential questions that related technological changes over time to history in general. Equally important, however, was the notion that the research that resulted in this project was actually part of the research for the larger paper requirement. This allowed a student to do two projects for the time-price of one.

Technology Unit Overview

What is technology?

How has technology changed over time?

How has changing technology affected the course of history?

How has technology affected the way we live?

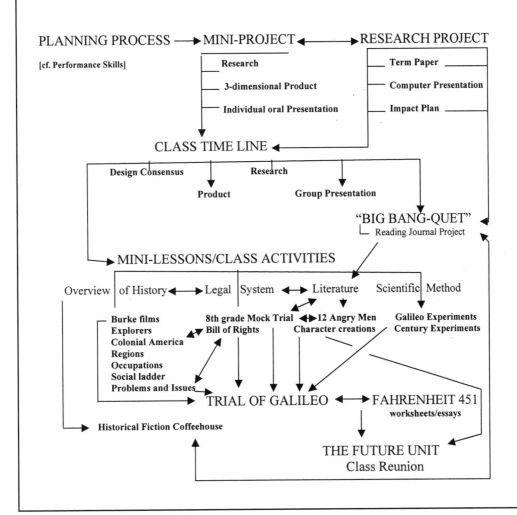

PLANNING PROCESS ⟶ MINI-PROJECT ⟷ RESEARCH PROJECT

[cf. Performance Skills]

— Research

— 3-dimensional Product

— Individual oral Presentation

— Term Paper

— Computer Presentation

— Impact Plan

CLASS TIME LINE

Design Consensus   Research

Product   Group Presentation

"BIG BANG-QUET"
└─ Reading Journal Project

MINI-LESSONS/CLASS ACTIVITIES

Overview | of History ⟷ Legal | System ⟷ Literature   Scientific | Method

Burke films
Explorers
Colonial America
Regions
Occupations
Social ladder
Problems and Issues

8th grade Mock Trial ⟷ 12 Angry Men
Bill of Rights   Character creations

Galileo Experiments
Century Experiments

TRIAL OF GALILEO ⟷ FAHRENHEIT 451
worksheets/essays

Historical Fiction Coffeehouse

THE FUTURE UNIT
Class Reunion

In reality, this arrangement allowed students to accomplish even more than that. During early unit planning discussions, we raised the issue of making a difference—the notion that Soundings was intended to give young adolescents an opportunity to be heard and to have a significant impact on their community. From this reminder came the idea of Footprints, or an impact plan. We asked each student to use her or his interest in the personal research topic as a pathway toward some form of community service, and some truly amazing service projects were conceived.

Two young ladies interested in art and in environmental issues respectively worked together to develop a "trash to art" program. They visited our two elementary schools, talked to the younger students about recycling, and recruited those students to make artworks out of discarded objects and materials. The pieces of "trash art" were then put on display.

Another young man, Erik, who was interested in agriculture, organized and produced an all-school talent show that raised several hundred dollars for the Farm Aid campaign that was active at that time. On a side note, this same young man saw a PBS special on No-Til farming as part of his research. That television show featured farmers who were using special satellite technology and No-Til techniques to raise crops while reducing runoff pollution into nearby waterways. The show focused on one farm from Africa, one from Asia, and one from the United States. When he learned that the American farm was located only an hour or so away from us, he got on the Internet, contacted

The initiative of one student enabled the entire class to visit a farmer who was experimenting with the No-Til technique.

the farmer, and arranged to take the entire Soundings class to that farm for a day to see firsthand how technology was changing agriculture.

I would have to say, however, that my personal favorite of the impact plans was the one titled Senior Surfers. This amazing service project was the brainchild of two Soundings students, one interested in computer technology and the other interested in gerontology. Together, these two girls visited the local senior center, interviewed the director, and asked if there was any way they could volunteer there, perhaps with the center's one or two computers. The director was a bit hesitant, not because she didn't want their help, but because, as she claimed, the senior citizens who came to the center didn't use the computers. Most had no idea about computers.

The girls immediately saw this as their opportunity and volunteered to teach the seniors how to use the computers. Returning to school, the girls talked to us, then to our principal, then to the computer room technicians, and got everyone's approval to reserve the computer lab for an hour each morning for four straight weeks. Then they returned to the senior center, advertised their idea, and soon had 15 to 20 senior citizens coming every day to the middle school computer room from 10 to 11 a.m.

The girls instructed the seniors in the basics of computer use such as word processing, Internet searching, and e-mail. As if this were not enough, the pair also visited a local coffee shop and convinced the owner that it would be great advertising, as well as a community service, if the shop would donate refreshments daily for the seniors. The owner agreed, and fresh coffee, tea, and bagels arrived every morning for the seniors.

Altogether, the students worked individually or in pairs to implement about 25 different Footprint projects that spring. Each impact plan grew directly out of the students' own research interests, and each performed a significant public service. The concept was a marvelous blend of the academic and real-world aspects of learning and made the rhetoric of curriculum integration an even greater reality.

The research paper also called for a blending of skills. As can be seen from the instruction sheet we eventually developed (pp. 111-112), in addition to the paper and the impact plan, the research project had, quite naturally, a technology component as well. The students were asked to summarize their research findings into a HyperStudio or PowerPoint presentation. This allowed them to accomplish many of the district's technology requirements without needing a separate computer class or computer project. Again, this is one of the advantages of curriculum integration: it reduces redundancy and increases cohesiveness, thus giving more meaning and context to every activity. Put bluntly, it can be an incredibly efficient and effective way to accomplish the impossibly numerous and repetitive standards put forward by the separate disciplines.

I think it is also important to say a word or two at this point concerning structuring a research project for young adolescents. While they may (or may not) have done reports in school before, it is doubtful that many will have done any real research. Thus, it is imperative that we help them through the process. We accomplished this in stages. First, the reader is aware by now that the entire program has been predicated on asking essential questions and then trying to find answers. So, in a very real sense, we start teaching research in the process of theme building. The medium is the message! On a second level, our first unit involved directed research projects. Though primarily conveyed in short paper and display formats, the process we put the students through is a preliminary form of research, and we discuss this with them. We debrief the steps, the results, and the pitfalls in preparation for the larger research project to come.

Finally, we set up the first research paper in a structured series of smaller steps that will help the students accomplish the larger goal. This idea is by no means original with me. In fact, I remember relying heavily years ago on a small booklet by Ross Burkhardt (1994), entitled *The Inquiry Process: Student-Centered Learning,* that gives detailed steps and forms. I adapted many of Ross's ideas to fit our needs and have further refined them over the past few years as we expanded the research requirement to two papers. The original research instruction sheets we used that first year follow on pages 111–113.

In year six, the original panel art work, which had been covered with cloth or paper for subsequent classes, was painted over for the new murals of outer space and under the sea.

Soundings 1999

Major Individual Research Project
Second Dimension: Technology

Name: _____

As part of our investigation into the ways technology affects our life, each of you will be responsible for an independent research project on a major topic of your choice.

This project will involve three basic, required parts:
1. A written term paper
2. A HyperStudio or PowerPoint computer presentation
3. An Action or Impact Component

Each of these has its own instructions outlined below.

I. The Term Paper, with   –footnotes
                              –history and development of area
                              –impact of technology
                              –major people, inventions, dates
                              –graphic representation of data/statistics

  A. This paper will answer the umbrella question
     "What impact has technology had on [your topic area]?"

  B. It must include the following sections

   1. A Cover Page with the title, your name, due date, and an illustration.

   2. An Introductory Section
      – identification and definition of the topic: statement of the issue
      – definition of technology
      – statement as to significance of the topic chosen and reason for choice; goal of report: questions trying to answer
      – overview of research processes and techniques employed

   3. A Background Section
      – history of the topic area: origins
      – early developments or conditions; early players
      – earliest forms of technology involved

   4. A Contemporary Conditions Section
      – What is currently happening in the topic field?
      – What has changed from the past?

continued

         – Data/statistics/charts/graphs/photos
         – Current players
         – Immediate effects
         – New technologies involved

5. Conclusions
         – Summary of answers to initial questions
         – Predictions for future

6. A Bibliography
         – Including print, electronic, and firsthand
           (interview) sources

C. This paper must include a minimum of ten (10) typed pages.

II. The HyperStudio or PowerPoint Presentation

  A. A presentation of the same basic information as the written paper in summary and more graphic form

  B. A preliminary graphic organizer or storyboard

III. An Action or Impact Component

  A. You need to develop a plan to share your research with others or to make a change in your topic area. For example:

    1. You might elect to teach a lesson to a class of younger children.
    2. You might devise a plan to solve a problem involved in your topic.
      a. Correspond with legislators about an important issue
      b. Recommend specific changes to a planning committee

  B. We'll discuss this with particular topics to help you clarify ideas.

Major Individual Research Project
Second Dimension: Technology

Name: _____

Project Plan and Due Dates

Requirement	Date Due	Completed
Topic Selection	Feb. 16	_____
List of Specific Research Questions	Feb. 18	_____
Preliminary Bibliography	Feb. 26	_____
Tentative Action/Impact Plan	March 10	_____
Rough Draft Introductory Section	March 10	_____
Rough Draft Background Section	March 25	_____
Graphic Organizer for HyperStudio/PowerPoint	April 28	_____
Complete Rough Draft	May 5	_____
Final Products	May 26	_____

Major Individual Research Project
Second Dimension: Technology

Name: _____

Project Plan Questions

I. How has technology affected _____?
(Your topic area)

II. Why is this an important area to explore?

III. List your four most important research questions that will guide you to an answer for Question I:

    A.

    B.

    C.

    D.

IV. For each of the questions in part III, list at least three specific questions you must answer:

    A. 1-3

    B. 1-3

    C. 1-3

    D. 1-3

One major change has been in the method used to establish the schedule within the project. That first year, after an overall target date was established, I broke the project down into the parts identified in the instruction form and set the various intermediate due dates. Over the years, I have worked more closely with the class to select intermediate due dates on the first paper, then I have left it up to each student on his or her own to set target due dates for the several steps along the process. This gives students the opportunity to try it for themselves, rather than relying on me or the class to set dates for them.

I have also learned that I need to help students with determining their thesis. They come up with good topic questions, but some of the students have trouble translating their question into an arguable thesis statement that will shape their paper and give it needed direction. So, I have included additional forms (pp. 115–117) used in subsequent years to help students gather input from peers. Again, many of these forms are adapted from Burkhardt's book (1994). The forms are condensed here. Ample room for the students to write their responses directly on the sheet is always provided when used.

The next form I use (p. 118) whenever there is an additional presentational component to the research paper. It is a front-and-back document condensed to one page here.

While the students worked on their research projects, presentations, and impact plans, my teaching partner and I were again charged with providing background information on the general trends of history and technological advancements. We found the James Burke videos from the *Connections* series to be immensely beneficial. Though difficult for some of the students to follow, the videos show quite dramatically how technology is a human endeavor motivated by very common needs and events, and often very interconnected in strange ways. We challenged ourselves, teachers and students, to diagram the course of connected events highlighted in each film, and then we reviewed our efforts afterwards. This helped all of us more clearly see the connections between history and technology that Burke had made. It also helped students with note-taking skills and the ability to listen to a presentation to cull the most important information. Of course, the films provide a marvelously memorable overview of history also.

Soundings

2005–2006

First Individual Research Project

Cutting Edge Technologies

As part of our investigation into cutting edge technologies, you are responsible for an independent research project on a topic of your choice. To formalize your research, we are asking that you prepare a short research paper.

The paper must include the following sections:

1. **A Cover Page** with the title, your name, due date, and an illustration.
2. **An Introductory Section**: (one page) identification and definition of the topic; statement of the primary research question; your **thesis** statement as to importance or significance of the topic chosen and reason for choice goals of research; major sub-questions you are trying to answer
3. **A Presentation of Researched Information Section (The Body):** (no set number) provide information and examples explaining answers to your questions; provide appropriate citations including any maps, charts, tables, diagrams, or illustrations.
4. **Conclusions**: (one page)
   Summary of answers leading to a conclusion regarding thesis question
   Predictions for future or suggestions for next steps/subsequent research
5. **A Bibliography/Sources Page:**
   Including print, electronic, and firsthand (interview) sources listed in proper format.

You must also turn in along with your final draft **all** preliminary instruction and planning sheets, outlines, and rough drafts in the folder provided. The rough and final drafts should be word processed in a clearly legible, standard 12-point font, double spaced (We recommend either Times New Roman, Times, or New York.) with one-inch margins. **Pages must be numbered.**

Structuring Your Project: Given the end due date of Wednesday, December 21, 2005, you must turn in the following items in the order and by the due dates listed below. Please note that there will be spot checks and intermittent progress reports between parts two and three, and between parts three and four.

	Due Date	Turned In	Teacher
1. **Preliminary planning sheets #1 and 2:**	Oct. 19		
2. **Rough draft of Introductory Section:**	Oct. 28		
3. **Outline of Presentation Section:**	Nov. 28		
4. **Rough draft of Presentation and Conclusions:**	Dec. 9		
5. **Draft of Bibliography/Sources Page**	Dec. 9		

Project Planning   1

Name:_____

Date: _____

Selecting Your Topic

Directions: From the list of questions we have generated on our first theme, select several questions that you find particularly interesting. (You may also include any new questions you may have thought of since we determined our topic.) List those questions here:

Are any of these questions directly related, suggesting a more encompassing research question, or does one of the questions strike you as a particularly good research question in and of itself? List that question here:

Why do you think this would make a good research topic question?

What do you expect or hope to learn by researching this topic?

Teacher Initials: _____

Date: _____

Project Planning   2

Name: _____

Date: _____

Inquiry Topic: _____

[Write your topic question from sheet #1]

Topic Questions

Directions: List at least ten important questions you have about your topic.

Teacher Initials: _____

Date: _____

Project Planning   3

Name: _____

Date: _____

Inquiry Topic: _____

Group Suggestions

Directions: Share your topic and starter questions with your table group. Record all the ideas, comments and questions they suggest. Do not judge or respond to these comments now; just write them down. Later, on the back of this sheet, you will review the list and select any ideas you think are appropriate for your research.

   Directions: (Back of sheet) Which of your table group's suggestions or questions do you think you will apply to your project? How might these help you in your research?

Teacher Initials: _____

Date: _____

Project Planning   4

Name: _____

Date: _____

Inquiry Topic: _____

Recording Sources

Directions: As you research your topic, you will be getting information from many sources. It is always important to keep track of these sources to avoid plagiarism and to relocate or verify information. Use this sheet to record your sources. Include pertinent information about the author, speaker or artist; publisher or producer; date of publication or interview; and any other information that helps identify your sources. Keep this sheet handy as you research. Be prepared to hand it in with your final project presentation. (Attach extra sheets as needed.)

Project Planning   5

Name: _____

Date: _____

Inquiry Topic: _____

Planning My Presentation

Directions: As you gather information about your topic, you should also begin to think about appropriate ways you could present the results of your research to the class. Use this form first to brainstorm presentation ideas, then to narrow the field.

List at least three (3) possible formats or media you think could appropriately convey your work to the class:

   1.

   2.

   3.

In light of your topic, your talents, and your strengths, what are the advantages and disadvantages of each possible format you listed?

	Advantages	Disadvantages
1.		
2.		
3.		

Discuss the advantages and disadvantages of each potential type of presentation with a friend. Get his or her opinion here: I think option #___ is the best choice because

Signed: _____

Which option have you decided to use? Why?

List all materials or resources you will need to make this type of presentation successful:

If your presentation is to be **other than** a written report or an oral report, please give a detailed outline or description of your ideas (attach extra pages if necessary).

Teacher Initials: _____ Date: _____

Our note-taking diagrams, together with the timelines we were making as we listened to the mini-project presentations, led rather naturally to a class decision to make another huge mural. Clearly a time line of technology made perfect sense. However, the students didn't want to paint over their first mural, so we decided to get a roll of primed canvas instead.

Findings from research done by small groups were depicted on large panels, which comprised a time line covering 13 centuries!

After several discussions, the class decided to divide into 13 groups. Each group would take one century from the 8th to the 20th centuries, research the technological advances and the general history of that century, and depict their findings on a 4' x 5' piece of canvas. We attached one-inch dowels to the top and bottom of each canvas panel so the panels could be suspended side by side to form the time line.

Then the group set about submitting possible designs of the time line's overall structure and appearance. A number were presented and discussed. Ultimately they chose one that would employ diagonal stripes, alternating on each panel, to give themselves the longest line for the chronology while still giving a connected appearance. Along the stripe, decades would be indicated and small illustrations of important people, historical events, and technological advances would be drawn. All of this would be superimposed on a representative painting from that century; for example, the Mona Lisa smiled enigmatically from behind the 16th century time line.

Beyond researching and painting its own time line panel, each group would be responsible for explaining it to the class. This would include reviewing the events illustrated, discussing their significance, and justifying their inclusion. The choice of the background work had to be explained, too, and its history given. Once again, this presentation method ensures that the group gets to share and celebrate its efforts, but it also ensures that the content is introduced and discussed by everyone in the class.

At the same time, we needed to make sure that the students learned about the scientific method, which was a required part of the eighth grade science curriculum in conventional classes. The Burke videos helped here, since the students got to see and hear how real scientists had set up their experiments and investigations. This also gave us the idea of connecting the scientific method to our big time line. After reviewing the steps of the scientific method, we asked the century groups to find through their research a particular type of issue that was being experimented with in their century. Here is what the instruction sheet eventually looked like:

Soundings   1999

Major Group Science Project. Second Dimension: Technology

Name: _____

As part of our investigation into the ways technology affects our life, you and your century group will be responsible for a science experiment project based loosely on your century.

This project will involve three basic, required parts:
1. Design and conduct an experiment using the scientific method to test a hypothesis in your assigned area.
2. Share your experiment with the class presentation in a 15-minute lesson that demonstrates or repeats the experiment.
3. Write up a lab report using the format attached.
    (Each of these has its own instructions outlined below.)

I. The Experiment:

   A. Discuss possible hypotheses and determine the one your group wishes to test.

   B. Design an experimental procedure to test the hypothesis. Include all the components as described on the lab report.

---

continued

C. Gather all the materials needed.

D. Conduct the experiment and record your observed results.

II. The Class Presentation:

A. Determine an appropriate strategy for sharing your experiment with the class. This strategy should involve the students as much as possible, and it must make clear all the required aspects of the experiment.

B. Gather materials needed, and work out the actual lesson plan. Submit this lesson plan to the teachers at least two (2) days BEFORE your assigned presentation date.

C. Present the lesson (no longer than 15 minutes) on your assigned date.

III. The Lab Report: Follow this format to prepare a lab report. **Each** student must turn in his or her own version.

Title

Your Name_____Date _____

Others in Group: _____

Background Observation:
[a description of the basic problem or issue you are trying to elucidate.]

Hypothesis: [The formal statement of your test question.]

Materials Involved: [List materials and amounts.]

Procedure: [Describe how you set up the experiment. Be sure to state controls and variables.]

Data: [Observations, results. May be narrative, statistical, or graphic.]

Conclusions and Recommendations:
Based on data gathered, summarize an answer to your hypothesis. Also outline possible future experiments or new questions raised by your work.

With these guidelines in hand, students proceeded to develop their own experiments, following the steps of the scientific method to demonstrate that issue to the class. We ended up dropping objects off the school roof, as an example, to test gravity and acceleration as Galileo had done. The students came up with the following list:

Century	Topic	Century	Topic
8th	water power/wheels	15th	vision/optics
9th	chemistry/alchemy	16th	color
10th	water resistance/ship hulls	17th	biology/ medicine
11th	magnetism/the compass	18th	botany/growth
12th	architectural techniques— arches	19th	light
13th	sound	20th	psychology
14th	wind power/sail design		

Each group had to work together to plan its experiment. This included submitting two forms for our review. The forms also helped us make sure we could get any materials or make any special arrangements a group might need to present its experiment. One group in particular, the 10th century group, needed a baby's wading pool for its experiment!

The important point, again, is the cohesiveness this establishes for the students. They see their learning not as discrete, separated bits of information, but as interconnected parts of a whole context. Because the information has this context and makes more sense, they remember more of it. How much of the material covered in schools is quickly and even rightfully forgotten within days, let alone months or years?

We had similar issues with language arts, for which we were to read a novel and a play, and for social studies, which required us to cover American history from the early explorers to the causes of the Civil War. In addition, the other eighth graders were covering the American court system and watching a mock trial put on by parent volunteers who were lawyers. We needed to account for all of these areas; and we wanted our students to learn, not merely cover the concepts involved. The trick was to find a way that connected all these areas in the context of the history of technology. We found, with the students' help, that we could do this, in part, by putting Galileo on trial.

When shown the district requirements from the subject areas, the class suggested we conduct a trial of our own. I suggested Galileo, because he had actually been tried, and that trial was directly related to scientific and technological issues. I further suggested that it might be fun to pick up on some of the people we had been learning about through our research and through the videos and to use Steve Allen's "Meeting of the Minds" approach. Since all of my students, and probably more than a few readers, are too young to remember this old television show from the days before HDTV or even color TV, "Meeting of the Minds" depicted hypothetical conversations among famous people who had lived in different places and eras. The class thought this would be fun as well as educational, so we drew up a list of about 50 or 60 famous people from all walks of life and all periods of history. The list included personalities from Bill Gates to Bill Shakespeare, Charlemagne to Charles Darwin, and Marie Curie to Margaret Meade. Obviously, Galileo was the defendant. Ben Franklin and Clarence Darrow became his defense team. They faced Plato and Tomás de Torquemada (a.k.a. the Grand Inquisitor of the Spanish Inquisition), the prosecuting attorneys representing Pope Urban VIII, the plaintiff. Buddha acted as our judge. All the remaining characters selected by the students would become either members of the jury or witnesses.

So every student chose a character. The final list of participants looked like this:

Galileo Galilei	Aristarchus of Samos	Pope Urban VIII
Plato	Tomás de Torquemada	Aristotle
Nicholas Copernicus	Socrates	Ferdinand Magellan
Ptolemy	Johannes Kepler	Isaac Newton
Christopher Columbus	Caroline Herschel	Mahatma Gandhi
Tycho Brahe	Queen Elizabeth I	William Shakespeare
Albert Einstein	Annie Jump Cannon	Mohammad
Benjamin Franklin	Thomas Jefferson	Saint Augustine
Clarence Darrow	Charles Darwin	Marie Curie
Siddhartha Gautama	Margaret Meade	Sigmund Freud
(Buddha)	ThomasEdison	Henry Ford
Marco Polo	Maria Montessori	Bill Gates
Leif Erikson	Indira Gandhi	Jeanne d'Arc
Martin Luther		

Students had to research the character chosen and determine how this character might have felt about Galileo, about scientific advancements, about the nature of the world, about the role of religion, about freedom of speech and press, and so on.

We gave them a guide sheet that looked like this:

The Trial of Galileo

Name: _____ Character: _____

Directions: Find out as much as you can about your character. Use the following questions as a guide to help you. Then think about how your character would react if he/she were called to testify (in a modern court) for or against Galileo and the heliocentric theory of the universe.

When and where did your character live?

What was the prevailing view of the universe at that time?

Why is your character famous? [Get as much information as possible so you can explain his/her accomplishments as if they were your own.]

Was your character particularly religious or philosophical? If so, what were his/her beliefs?

[Again, know these well enough to speak about them as if they were your own.]

What did your character look like? How did he/she dress? (Think about a costume!)

What did other people say and think about your character when he/she was alive?

What have people said or thought about your character since his/her death?

What would your character think about Galileo as a person?

What would your character think about the heliocentric theory of the universe?

What would your character think about Galileo's attempts to prove and spread this theory?

They wrote up their findings in short papers that we put together into a booklet we titled *The Trial of the Century: A Who's Who*. The students had to determine what type of personality the famous person most likely had and how they could, in essence, bring that character back to life through speech and mannerisms. They also had to come up with an appropriate costume or prop.

To help them with characterization, we read Rose's (1981) *Twelve Angry Men* out loud together. We went over the roles and procedures of our court system, and the attorneys conducted the *voir dire,* interviewing each character in turn. That was how the jury was selected. The attorneys then divided the remaining characters into witnesses for the prosecution or the defense, depending on the testimony in the *voir dire* and the descriptions in the *Who's Who* booklet.

Costuming was just one part of the comprehensive study made of the individual characters.

The trial turned out to be an outstanding experience for everyone. What is more, it showed once again how many apparently disparate threads of knowledge could be successfully woven into a colorful fabric of learning. The students learned about our legal system, about many important historical figures, and about character development as a literary skill. The learning was firsthand and actively participatory, yet it was clearly rigorous by any academic standards.

We extended this fabric even further as we read Bradbury's (1991) *Fahrenheit 451* together as a class. This novel illustrates social and personal conflicts surrounding governmental censorship and restrictions on knowledge—precisely the issue involved in Galileo's case. This afforded the students a chance to experience the same concepts from the literary perspective, as it also allowed us to help them learn how to read closely and analyze a novel. It was a perfect fit.

We handled the additional social studies responsibilities with respect to American history from the period of exploration up to the Civil War in a somewhat different way. However, we also tried to maintain direct connections with our other activities. The reader will recall that many of our characters in the trial of Galileo were explorers like Magellan and Columbus, or early American statesmen, like Jefferson and Franklin. As we examined these characters, we were clearly able to refer directly to the American history standards at that time. Similarly, many of the James Burke videos referenced historical events as well as figures from the period in question.

Effective oral comunication—acting—was one of the skills developed in this comprehensive project.

Beyond that, we devised a couple of specific activities that linked American history with our interest in technology. First, we divided the class into three new groups. Each group assumed responsibility for one section of colonial America. They were given a guide sheet that looked like the one on p. 127.

As is clear from the guide sheet, each group researched a region, put together a presentation, and then shared information with the class. To help with their research, our shared readings were overview materials from American history texts. We also reviewed the U. S. Constitution, which for a few years was part of the summer packet reading. (It was later dropped from the summer packet when the eighth grade social studies curriculum changed from American History to a survey of the ancient world.) These readings gave everyone some common background and fundamental information. Students included some of this information on our individual and painted time lines.

During the subsequent regional presentations, my teaching partner and I focused attention and discussion on the different ways technology affected the three regions. Ultimately, this led us into some significant discussions concerning the causes of the Civil War, which was a major part of the eighth grade social studies curriculum.

In a similar way, following these regional presentations and discussions, we asked each student to select an occupation that was important to his or her region during the colonial period. The students had a day or two to find out about that occupation with respect to the technology involved, the education required, the compensation earned, and the social status granted. We next leaned two long strips of wood against the wall to form the legs of a ladder, and we gave each student a strip of poster board about 18" long and 2" wide. Students wrote their occupation on this piece of cardboard and illustrated it with a symbol, much as colonial merchants created signs to indicate the nature of their business. As each student presented his or her information, we literally constructed a social ladder depicting the intricate societal relationships of that era.

Soundings   **1999**

Colonial America
Group Mini-Presentation

Name_____   Group: New England   Mid-Atlantic   Southern

Directions: You and your group are to find out as much as you can about the colonial region assigned to you. Your group must provide information to the rest of us on the topics listed below. Use a map and visuals to make your mini-presentation interesting as well as informative.

1. Which colonies comprise your region?

2. Where is each located?

3. When was each established?

4. By whom (nationality and/or group) was each established?

5. For what reason(s) was it established?

6. Who were the leaders and important historical figures in these colonies?

7. What difficulties and/or conflicts did each colony experience?

8. Describe the geographic/topographic/climatic conditions of your region and explain how these factors affected the development of the colonies.

9. Describe the agriculture and industry of the region.

10. Describe the lifestyle of the colonists in your region. What made them different from the colonists in the other regions?

Once again, I want to emphasize the point that standards and external requirements do not have to be viewed as roadblocks. They may, at times, make things more difficult, but just as often they can make it more interesting by providing opportunities for students to make connections. That is both the challenge and the joy of learning, and it is more likely to occur for students in an integrated curriculum than those in a traditionally segregated curriculum, because curriculum integration intentionally focuses on such connections.

We were able to connect the students' own questions and interests with the school's requirements in a seamless way that made sense to the students. A look at Appendix 5 (p. 196) shows just how thoroughly we did address standards, more than required, in just this one unit. Were we to add in those covered in the first unit, The Big Bang, virtually all the major standards for grades seven through nine would have had extensive attention. To the students, however, the more important point was the way all this led to the Big Bang-quet and, eventually, to the final unit on the future.

Students sharing their learning with adults is always a part of major studies in Soundings.

For the Big Bang-quet, the students once again took over the activities center for a day and an evening. They hung their time line panels in chronological order along one wall. They had table seating for over 200 people, and each table had a centerpiece made by students from recycled techno-trash—items like old movie reels, cassette and cartridge tapes, pieces of broken computers. Around the circumference of the room, the students set up display tables to show off their research projects and showcase their impact plans.

Students planned a general potluck menu and divided among themselves responsibilities for salads, casseroles, breads, beverages, and desserts. They invited our school district superintendent to be the keynote speaker, and asked him to talk specifically about changing technology at the high school and how it would affect their education in the next four years.

They also invited their parents, all our other district and building administrators, all the people who had helped them in their research, and even many of the people they had helped with their impact plans— people like our senior surfers.

The Radnor Middle School
SOUNDINGS Program

Welcomes you to our

BIG BANG-Quet
Celebrating our study of Technology
* * * *

Evening's Festivities

6:00 p.m.	Time to view students' displays
7:00 p.m	Greetings and opening remarks
7:05 p.m	Dr. John A. DeFlaminis
	"What the Future May Hold"
7:20 p.m	Dinner and good conversation
8:00 p.m	Introduction of guests

The evening was a wonderful celebration of their accomplishments and validation of their learning. Guests were amazed and impressed; the students were exuberant and proud. I suppose we could be tempted to credit the evening's success to the magic of technology, but I believe it really was the result of empowering young adolescents to take charge of their learning.

After we debriefed the Big Bang-quet, the class moved on to its third and final unit, The Future. The reader may have noticed that this unit was actually shown on the technology schematic (p. 107). This is because the students decided to make their third unit flow directly from the second. Since the theme of this unit was "What might my life be like in the future?" it made sense to the students to project themselves into the year 2020, when they would all be young adults. It made further sense to assume for the sake of the unit that their strong interest in a particular area—the same interest that had given substance to their research project and impact plan—would by 2020 be part of their life's work.

With this in mind, the students elected to project their area of research into the future. Using research into the current trends and issues in their chosen field, each student wrote a short paper on possible future trends and issues in that area. In addition, they described what sort of occupation they might be pursuing relative to that field in 2020.

To make this short three-week study more personal and more interesting, the students wanted to act out their future. We decided to hold a Soundings reunion, 2020. Each student wrote up a hypothetical autobiography, incorporating some of the information from his or her paper on the future. My teaching partner and I photocopied these, but we omitted all names. The class received copies to read through before the reunion. Then we created a scavenger hunt of sorts using details and extensions of these autobiographies.

At the reunion, the students went around talking with each other, trying to discover which student matched each clue. In the process, we all learned a lot about possible futures in different lines of endeavor; and we had a lot of fun with all the "personal" stories as well. The reunion served as a marvelous culminating experience for the year because it tied together their themes and focused on them as individuals and a learning community.

Looking back over that year, even now, a number of years later, I continue to smile with satisfaction at the incredible levels of academic and personal accomplishment these students achieved that year. Checking back against the school's requirements and standards, these students clearly met or exceeded virtually all of them. I would further argue that they did so to a greater extent than students in a conventional curriculum.

They will remember what they learned far longer than their traditionally schooled peers because they owned the learning.

CHAPTER EIGHT

The Reality Proves the Rhetoric

An important characteristic of SOUNDINGS is that we are given opportunities to experiment with a different learning method, the firsthand learning experience, which supplies us with not only knowledge for school, but knowledge for life.　　　—Jordan E.

Having read about the Soundings I experiences in some detail, the reader should have a clear idea of how curriculum integration actually looks when the theory is put into practice—and the rhetoric becomes reality. Was year one unusual? No. Every Soundings class since then has demonstrated the same sort of enthusiasm and determination. Their questions have been similar in many respects, but each class has approached their questions in very unique ways. The students have demonstrated repeatedly that they could and would perform admirably and successfully when given the opportunity to take charge of their own education. Summaries of all the themes carried out from the second through the seventh years of Soundings are found in Appendix 6 (p. 212). The variety, depth, and quality of the studies undertaken by students in Soundings readily become apparent when one reviews these summaries.

All fine, well, and good, some would say; but how can we prove Soundings students have in fact learned as well as their peers in the conventional curriculum? Anecdotal evidence is nice, but what "hard" data can we offer to substantiate the claim that curriculum integration is a more effective form of education?

First, while I emphasize once again my general dislike of standardized tests, my students nevertheless endure them each year, just like their counterparts in the regular curriculum. As we see in Figure 1, results from one of these tests given in some years of the Soundings program have consistently shown little or no statistical difference in test scores.

FIGURE 1

SOUNDINGS ERB WRITING TEST RESULTS COMPARED TO THOSE OF THE ENTIRE GRADE								
Class = Soundings Years not presented in chronological order to maintain anonymity								
School = All Grade 8								
Year		Overall Develop- ment	Organi- zation	Support	Sentence Structure	Word Choice	Mechanics	Total Raw Score	Scale Score
	Class	4.5	4.6	4.6	4.4	4.4	4.3	26.8	873.7
X	School	4.4	4.5	4.3	4.2	4.3	4.2	25.9	843.6
	Class	4.4	4.6	4.2	4.2	4.1	4.1	25.5	865.2
X	School	4.4	4.5	4.3	4.2	4.2	4.2	25.7	874.6
	Class	4.1	4.4	3.8	4.1	4.1	4.1	24.5	845
X	School	4.1	4.2	3.9	3.9	4.1	4.0	24.2	827

In some years, averaged scores for Soundings students top the average of regular students by a tenth of a point or two; some years the reverse is true. However, the differences either way are always statistically insignificant. The same can be said of student scores on the Pennsylvania System of School Assessment (PSSA) tests our eighth graders are required to take each year. In other words, though we do not teach in a conventional way or cover a prescribed curriculum, our students still do as well on conventional tests as other students. Clearly, curriculum integration is not inhibiting our students' abilities to succeed on high-stakes standardized tests.

Clearly, curriculum integration is not inhibiting our students' abilities to succeed on high-stakes standardized tests.

The reader may further rest assured that were this not the case, the Radnor Township School District would not permit the program to continue. The district maintains an academic reputation second to none. We compete for students with one of the nation's highest concentrations of elite private schools, which is why our students take the Educational Records Bureau (ERB) writing test in addition to the PSSA tests. What is more, our high school prides itself on sending 90-plus percent of our graduates on to colleges and universities. If any program of studies were to jeopardize that reputation or any students' ability to succeed, the administration would move quickly to amend or end it. The fact that Soundings is now into its 8th year as this book comes out—and its precursor, Watershed, is now in its 20th year—ought to make it clear that this method works—academically!

Nevertheless, our greatest struggle in the early years of the Soundings program was convincing parents that they would not be jeopardizing their children's collegiate prospects by allowing them to participate in a non-conventional curriculum. Ironically, this parental concern has turned out to be another positive indicator of our success. Each year parents of Soundings students express satisfaction and pleasure with the results their children achieve in the program. One father, for example, wrote to his daughter on her last biweekly self-assessment in May of 2005, "It's been fun watching you do so well and be so enthusiastic about your year in Soundings." To which the mother added, "We are so pleased with B.'s year in Soundings!" Another parent that same spring reported, "M. has grown tremendously through the course of this year. She has gained a greater appreciation of her strengths and has clearly been able to identify the areas she needs to work on." Yet another father said of his son, "We are proud of J. Soundings was the right decision. He had a great year. Thank you." I have file drawers full of such comments. Here are a few more:

> B. is working harder and at a more sophisticated level this year—
> and really benefiting from it, although it definitely pushes her.
> —D. B. (mother) 4/1/03

> Soundings was a perfect match for K. and all her interests. She has
> learned so much—in numerous ways. —J. O. (mother) 4/29/03

> C. does well because he is inspired to do so. He really enjoys the
> "Soundings" way. I am proud of him also. —D. F. (mother) 3/5/02

He has truly been enjoying these projects and learning experiences. This year has been another period of growth in an unusual and beneficial educational format. —N. P. (Mother) 5/28/02

I think if she did 8th grade Soundings for the next 3 or 4 years she might qualify as an official assistant—we could save a lot of money on college! —C. R. (mother) 3/12/02

And my personal favorite, a sentiment expressed countless times:

Does the year really have to end? —J.J. (mother) 5/20/02

Again, this is but a sampling of the positive comments we receive from parents each year. To me they are all the verification I need that the program is working. It is interesting to note as well that in all the years of the Soundings program, only one child has been withdrawn; and that was in October of the very first year when we were just getting started. Since then, no parents have requested their child be removed and placed back into the regular curriculum. This fact, together with the universally positive feedback we get from parents, lets us know that the concept is sound.

Jeu Hee, like others, recognized the many pluses of Soundings.

And of course the students themselves let us know directly. In May of 2005, Beth wrote, "No words can describe how much I have enjoyed this year in Soundings! I have learned so much and I am going to miss Soundings so much! I am so glad I had this opportunity for eighth grade." Another of her classmates, Jeu Hee, said, "I'm really sad this year [has] only a couple months left until the end of the year. I hope to exert my best to finish off the year! I love Soundings! I feel like it's really helped me speak up more and work harder."

In addition to maintaining a file of such comments, we have tried to follow our students' progress as they have entered high school. Though once again not my favorite way of assessing students, grades are viewed by many parents and by the society at large as an indicator of success. So we have tried to look at the first quarter grades of our alumni to see if they are succeeding in this respect at the high school. Most years we are able to obtain copies of only our own students' first quarter grades. These have consistently shown that our students do well reentering a more traditional curriculum. Students who struggled with self-discipline or self-motivation, those few who never "caught on" to the Soundings philosophy, tend to struggle again in high school. The greater majority who did internalize the Soundings philosophy has tended to do well at the high school. We see very few failing grades among our population; and, interestingly, the few "Fs" we do see are usually in mathematics and world languages, neither of which fall under the Soundings purview.

One year we were able to obtain the first quarter grade point averages for the entire freshman class. This enabled us to compare directly Soundings students' performance to that of the students from the regular program. Figure 2 clearly shows Soundings students on average performed as well as or better than their peers.

FIGURE 2
**First Quarter GPA Comparisons, Soundings
vs. Entire Freshmen Class**

Percent of Class by GPA, Autumn 2003

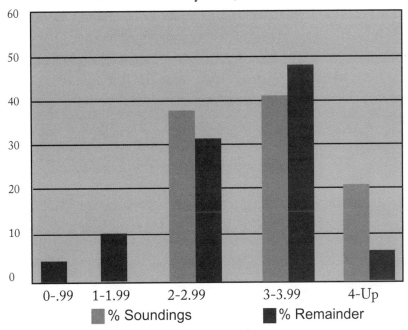

Data Set for Figure 2

GPA RANGE	# Students	% Soundings	# Students	% Remainder
0-.99	0	0	7	2.8
1-1.99	0	0	25	10
2-2.99	15	38.4	79	31.9
3-3.99	16	41	120	48.5
4-Up	8	20.5	16	6.4

As the chart and data illustrate, no Soundings student received a grade point average below 2.0 for the first semester at the high school, whereas close to 13% of the remaining freshman class did fail to attain at least the 2.0 level. What is more, while percentages of both groups receiving a GPA in the 2-to-3 point range is relatively equal, a significantly higher percentage of Soundings students scored in the 4-and-up range. In fact, though Soundings students represented only 14% of the entire freshman class, they accounted for 33% of the students receiving the highest GPAs that year. These figures show clearly that Soundings students adjusted very well to the demands of high school academics.

In the fall of 2005, we were able to obtain specific grades for former Soundings students in the freshman class, along with grade distributions by courses for the entire ninth grade class. From these data we extrapolated the following information:

FIGURE 3

First Quarter GPA Comparison by Subject: Soundings Alumni and Freshman Class, Autumn 2005

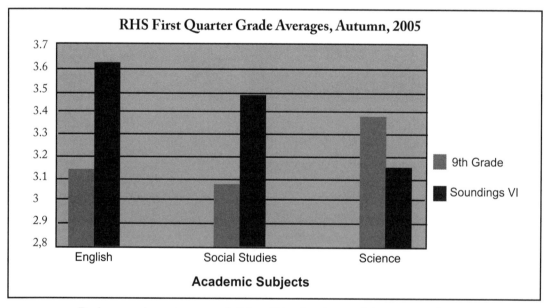

Radnor students in general did well in the three subject areas of English, social studies, and science, with average GPAs above 3.0 in each subject. Within that generally high level of academic performance across the board, note that Soundings students that year substantially outperformed their peers in two of the three subjects, while still making an admirable showing in the third.

A well-constructed program using curriculum integration prepares students for the rigors of high school at least as well as a conventional program—while simultaneously meeting the other needs of young adolescents to a much higher degree than conventional curricula.

Though we have not received comparative data for students from every year of the program, we have had no indication from the high school that the years reported here are in any way atypical or abnormal. As with standardized test score data, numbers may fluctuate in minor ways from year to year; however, the main point these data so clearly illustrate is that a well-constructed program using curriculum integration prepares students for the rigors of high school at least as well as a conventional program—while simultaneously meeting the other needs of young adolescents to a much higher degree than conventional curricula. The abundant opportunities Soundings purposefully provides for students to work in groups, to make formal presentations, to explore interests, to take the initiative, and to offer leadership, help them immeasurably in identifying their own talents and skills and developing socially as distinctive personalities. Soundings students will meet well the broad goals of the middle level school as set forth in *Turning Points* (1989).

> Our 15-year-old will be: an intellectually reflective person, a person en route to a lifetime of meaningful work, a good citizen, a caring and ethical individual, and a healthy person. (p. 15)

Thus, while impressive as evidence of success in the conventional sense, none of the numerical data captures the greatest successes of Soundings students in achieving the broader goals of an education identified above. Their growth as young people who possess confidence and a desire to learn is not measured quantitatively on a standardized test. Their creativity and their sense of community cannot be contained by graphite-filled bubbles on computer paper. To assess this type of growth, one has to talk directly to adults who work with these students in subsequent years.

One veteran ninth grade teacher, Jeanne Lynam, had this to say about the Soundings students with whom she has worked:

> *Our Soundings students tend to be articulate and most willing to express their ideas in class. They are facilitators when it comes to class discussions in both initiating discussion and building on others' ideas.*

They are self-motivated and very self-confident. Because they have been allowed to discover their own interests in the classroom, they are more "driven" to pursue those interests in the high school learning environment, especially one that encompasses a broad curriculum, such as the multidisciplinary program that I have taught for a number of years. I feel that the greatest asset of these students is their passion for learning. They learn for learning's sake and not for the grade alone.

Jeanne has another, deeper perspective on this type of learning because her eldest daughter participated in the Watershed Program its very first year. According to Jeanne, "Our daughter matured more in one year than I would ever have expected. She loved the course and all of its opportunities and I really believe that the challenges presented that year gave birth to her passion for knowledge and learning. She has a master's degree from Duke, a love for reading all things, and an amazing ability to be undaunted in the face of obstacles." As both a teacher and a parent, Jeanne has witnessed and identified the positive benefits of student-centered curriculum integration.

And she is not alone. Another veteran high school teacher, Fran F., when asked how former Soundings students were handling the transition to high school, put it this way:

Eleven of the kids in our Integrated Themes class and one in my college-prep class had Soundings. The eleven are some of the best discussants we have ever had; they are kind to each other and very good listeners as well. I asked them to write some comments about things they learned in Soundings. I'll excerpt some as follows:

1. *able to do long-term projects*
2. *lots of major writing assignments*
3. *ways of researching (citing sources)*
4. *focus questions*
5. *discussion skills*
6. *exploration of how I learn best and what I need to do to research*
7. *helped me realize what I have to do to remember information*
8. *gave me the freedom to explore what study options worked best without worrying about getting a bad grade.*

Best of all, of course, are the assessments of the students themselves. For example, I received this unsolicited e-mail example from a former Soundings student after he completed his freshman year:

I wanted to write to you at the end of my first year at high school in order to tell you how much the Soundings program prepared me for it, and how far I have come because of Soundings. I have read 27 books this year as opposed to last year's 20, and I owe it all to Soundings, where you ignited the joy of reading for me and I cannot thank you enough for that. Also, Soundings prepared me for high school much more than I would have thought at the beginning of the year. The way we learned to work in Soundings made working in a regular classroom much easier. Soundings was such a great experience and I am sure that it will stand to be the best school year that I will ever have. Also, if you ever need me to recommend the program at one of the meetings, feel free to send me an e-mail.

Sincerely, Alex G.

Merritt J., who recently graduated from our high school, has frequently volunteered to share his Soundings experiences with audiences of parents, students, and teachers. In fact, he has even spoken at the National Middle School Association's conference. This past spring he sent along to this year's Soundings students his comments about his transition to high school. Here are some excerpts from that letter:

The integrated programs at Radnor Middle School made me excited to be learning and interested in what I was studying. Soundings allowed me to study what I was interested in through incorporating my interests into the curriculum that the class chose for that year. I incorporated my personal interest in environmental issues into the topics we studied by focusing on the effects of civil conflict on the environment when we studied violence, and how environments shape societies when we studied cultures. In Soundings I wrote the two longest research papers I have written to this date, and I am a senior in high school. …

Everyone is allowed to work at whatever academic pace suits him or her, but everyone is pulled along by their peers. I learned an immense amount about working in groups with different types of people, with different motivations, strengths, and weaknesses. … Most of my friends found very little difficulty in transferring from Soundings to high school. The hardest transition of all was returning to scheduled (and for the most part boring) classes. …

Overall, I felt that Soundings was a fantastic experience. I was allowed to study what I was interested in, and learned more that year than in any other year of my education. Also, I had more fun in the integrated programs at the middle school than I have had in any structured academic program. Soundings was a great experience for me, and I am very happy I participated in such a wonderful program. I wish that my other classes could have been as educational and meaningful as Soundings was for me.

Similarly, at the close of her freshman year, Katie G. reflected back on her Soundings and her subsequent high school experiences. Here is part of what she had to say:

When I first walked into Soundings, I was very nervous about being in a new and unique environment. However, as the year progressed, I began to learn and become a strong, independent person. The Soundings experience allowed me to become more confident and responsible. . . .

Last year I was worried that because I did not have structured tests and quizzes that I would be unprepared for high school. However, Soundings showed me how to relax and manage my time. This year I was fully prepared for any test or quiz a teacher gave. Being part of Soundings helped me achieve so much! Best of all, I became the person I wanted to be. Soundings has taught me so many things and is something I will never forget.

Reflections and testimonials such as these clearly show that students in curricular programs like Soundings go on to successful high school careers. They view themselves as prepared and confident in their abilities. What is more, the lessons they master about democracy, about fairness, about social justice, and about working together transcend grade point averages and stanines.

Dr. Dave Brown, a professor at nearby West Chester University who visits Soundings regularly with undergraduate middle school teacher education students, provided this informal assessment of Soundings from these pre-service teachers.

These future teachers have read about curriculum integration but usually express a general disbelief that students and teachers could design a learning experience that provides young adolescents with so much responsibility for their own learning.

As we sit among the Soundings students, I usually start with a general first question for the Soundings students. The question draws hand waving among the students who are eager to respond—and are more than adequate in doing so. As the questions and answers continue, my students begin to believe that these eighth graders are responsible for creating their own curriculum, engaging in research processes, experiencing critical reading and writing, and presenting their findings to others throughout the year.

When we need to leave and we file out of the building into the parking lot, I always stop there and ask if they want to make any comments before we leave. Semester after semester, I hear the same first comment from several students almost at once: "Those are the smartest eighth grade students I've ever seen." I want to laugh because I know something every pre-service middle level teacher needs to know. The Soundings integrated curriculum program provides these eighth graders with the cognitive tools to grow into responsible lifelong learners in ways that no prescribed curriculum can ever accomplish.

Another regular visitor, Dr. Nancy Doda of National-Louis University, offered these assessments growing out of her experience plus the findings of a research study that included Soundings students.

Over a period of eight years, I have invited dozens of my graduate students, middle school teachers, principals, superintendents, and even school board members to join me in visiting Soundings. Each and every year, those that do, including myself, are stunned by the nature and high quality of the learning they witness. Most report that having seen the Soundings learning experience firsthand, they will never again be able to conceive of "best" middle school education as they once did.

The most profound window into the impact of the Soundings learning experience is found in the actions and voices of the students who acknowledge their very own transformation and growth. And, it is easy to see why students claim such ownership. On any ordinary day, students are actively at work: leading class discussions and presentations, conducting team or individual research, preparing final products, or actively debating in small groups how best to proceed to accomplish shared goals. On one occasion, when the students were asked by a visitor why they worked so hard when they did not receive letter grades, the astute eighth grader gently explained: "We don't want to let each other down." This of course generated a host of related questions regarding how the two Soundings teachers managed to get kids to feel this way about their work and each other.

Since these students are exceedingly comfortable sharing their thinking, students are always ready to elaborate. One student gave the visitors a deeper look at the way relationships in the Soundings team took shape with these comments:

"At the start of the year we created the themes we are going to study, so right from the start we had to really think together, listen to each other and learn to be a group. We also developed our own rules, which can change things too. …We did activities in which we were constantly having to work together. This really was different from my other classes. I saw that I was never really all alone and so now we stick together."

During the past two years, Trudy Knowles and I collected data from middle school students across North America. We asked students to respond in writing to the prompt: "What should middle school teachers know about middle school students?" After analyzing over 2,700 unedited responses, we discovered that one collection of responses was dramatically different. In this group, responses addressed issues that were largely ignored by students in the larger sample. We traced these unique responses to the Soundings students.

The Soundings students' quotes were distinguishable from nearly all other quotes collected, with the exception of students in the few other similarly democratic classroom settings. They were more articulate and sophisticated in their thinking. Only these students connected schooling with life, expressed concern for student voice and choice, and acknowledged how they had come to treasure the power of their own learning. Something profoundly transformative occurs for young people in the Soundings learning experience.

Dr. K. Ann Renninger of Swarthmore College has taken students in both her educational psychology and child psychology classes and honors seminars to observe and study Soundings.

The experience of studying the Soundings program provides my students with a model of how a democratic classroom with an integrated curriculum can work and has allowed them to map findings from current research on learning to classroom practice (e.g., the importance of students' developing understanding and acquiring skills through reflection and work with meaningful tasks).

Findings from a series of studies that my students and I have conducted will be reported in more detail elsewhere, but let me provide an overview here.

Over two different years of the Soundings program, we studied student learning and motivation in the Soundings classroom. We were particularly interested in whether all of the students in the classroom were benefiting, or if perhaps it had more of an impact on some groups of students than on others. In particular, we wondered whether student motivation and learning would be influenced by their gender, standardized testing, prior experience in an alternative classroom, and/or student "fit" to the classroom, their readiness to be in a classroom that involved taking responsibility for themselves as a learner.

Interestingly, we found that all students were benefiting from their participation in the Soundings program: they all engage in the different types of activities of the classroom, and their written work reflects changed capacity when work from the beginning of the year is compared to that of the end of the year. Briefly, these changes include both developments in their mechanical skills and their abilities to make meaningful connections to the subject matter covered. Not surprisingly, perhaps, Soundings students also appear to make an easy transition to high school. Alumni of the Soundings program, for example, recounted during interviews that they made the transition to high school with a skill set that included confidence about themselves as learners that they had not all experienced prior to their year in Soundings. They reported that they developed their abilities to take risks and be resourceful as learners, and they thought that they were more likely than non-Soundings peers to ask questions of others and to find the resources they needed to do work that was assigned.

Interviews with Soundings students and a group of control students (eighth graders who had not been in the Soundings program; students whose year-end goals for content learning were the same as those of the Soundings students), furthermore, suggested that while both groups of students spent an equal amount of time doing homework for their classes, their motivation for school and homework differed significantly. Soundings students, echoing the alumni who were interviewed, said that they knew that they were doing well since they tracked their own progress in their self-assessments. They felt prepared for high school and that their study skills had improved over the year, citing their problem-solving abilities, organization, reading comprehension, ability to work with feedback, and note taking. Control students, on the other hand, reported that they knew how they were doing by looking at their grades. They thought that they were prepared for high school too, and cited gains in note taking over the year as critical. Soundings students reported that their future was their motivation for working hard, citing their parents and the importance of feeling accomplished. Control students cited parents and grades as the reason that they worked hard in school.

Of importance in the comparison of the interviews of the Soundings students to the control students is the finding that the views of the Soundings students did not vary based on gender, standardized achievement scores, prior alternative classroom experience, or fit to the class. In fact, observations in the classroom over an 8-week period suggest that all students are engaged and constructively involved as learners in whole group, small group, and individual work. Differences among groups emerged in terms of when students engaged in particular behaviors. Thus, for example, some students were more likely to ask questions in the whole group, others in the small group, and others in seat work.

Findings such as these suggest that students will seriously engage in and begin to take responsibility for pursuing learning when the disciplinary content is meaningful. While some students may have been more ready for a Soundings-type classroom when they entered the class at the beginning of the year, all students progressively developed the skills and productive disposition that enabled them to be learners who can achieve both in Soundings and post-Soundings.

These additional assessments should convince skeptics that a democratic, student-centered program using integrative curriculum fulfills all major objectives of middle level education in an exemplary fashion.

Is it a perfect program? Of course not. I learn more and more each year, and see new ways to improve the program and increase student empowerment. I have also come to realize how much one of my own caveats applies to Soundings. The reader will recall from Chapter 2 how I warned that the results of any system vary with the degree to which the system is fully implemented. As I see what Soundings students accomplish each year, I become all the more painfully aware of the limitations we still place upon them as we try to fit the Soundings approach into the traditional school. I can only dream about the achievements students would experience if they and the Soundings system still were not shackled by limitations imposed by the traditional curriculum and, in this day and age, by intrusive legislation and the misguided "businessification" of education in America.

Indeed, I have been struck in recent months by a number of sources I've encountered outside the sphere of progressive education circles—sources that have been either intentionally or inadvertently singing a similar tune. For example, in his best-selling book, *The World Is Flat*, Thomas Friedman (2005) describes the needs of the 21st century workplace as very different from those of the 20th century. The modern, flat world workplace will call for levels of collaboration and creativity unlike anything seen to this point. To prepare for this, students will definitely need a wealth of background knowledge. However, according to Friedman, it is apparent that they will need more than traditional knowledge: "Being adaptable in a flat world, knowing how to 'learn how to learn,' will be one of the most important assets any worker can have" (p. 239). Learning how to learn, or, as our current superintendent likes to say, "Learning how to figure out what to do next when you don't know what to do next," does not come about through rote memorization of "Trivial Pursuit" facts. It does not spring from drill and kill worksheets or from taking notes on lectures followed by verbatim regurgitation. If we want to prepare students for a 21st century workplace, we cannot continue to rely on the 19th century factory model of education still in vogue and being perpetuated in reaction to NCLB.

Alvin Toffler (2006), in a recent interview about his new book, *Revolutionary Wealth*, echoed this sentiment when he asserted:

> Our current school system is based on factory-style disciplines. Children are marched through a sequence of standard-length classes with metronomic regularity. Learning is almost always by rote and repetitive. That is simply out of sync with today's emergent work environments. To succeed and create value in much of the workplace today, you need to be creative and a self-starter. You must be able to take responsibility for your own time and work independently. (p. 8)

Study after study over the last 75 years has shown that creativity, independent thinking, self-motivation, self-discipline, and cooperation are all skills that can and must be taught and nurtured. The teaching and nurturing of these skills cannot occur effectively in an institutionalized system that emphasizes competition, compartmentalization, fragmentation, and failure—hallmarks of the present system. Want proof? Spend some time in any traditional school.

What is more, the NCLB legislation is exacerbating an already dismal situation. As interviewees in several recent *New York Times* online articles have pointed out, "Many of the tests that states are introducing under NCLB contain many questions that require students merely to recall and restate facts, rather than do more demanding tasks like applying or evaluating information" (Winerip, 2006). Because these tests entail such high stakes and severe consequences if Adequate Yearly Progress targets are not met (and these targets virtually guarantee some failure for even the best of schools) "many schools that once offered rich curriculums" are now "systematically trimming courses like social studies, science and art. A nationwide survey by a nonpartisan group … indicates that the practice, known as narrowing the curriculum, has become standard procedure in many communities" (Winerip, 2006). The result will clearly be an entire generation of students who have been quite literally drilled to mental death and who possess no full understanding of the world into which they are released upon graduation. Their NCLB-certified diploma will perhaps attest to their ability to read and calculate, but will simultaneously represent a dearth of both the background knowledge and the thinking skills they will need to survive in the 21st century.

Upon reflection, one has to wonder just what the real motives behind NCLB truly are. An April 2006 Queue, Inc. *U.S. Education News* article online asserted, "This year, the Assessment, Tutoring and Test Preparation Services, and Supplemental Content markets saw the most dramatic revenue acceleration in response to 'No Child Left Behind' (NCLB) mandates, according to Eduventures' recently released annual state-of-the-industry report, entitled, *K-12 Solutions Learning Markets and Opportunities*." The article goes on to predict a continuing rise in revenue for "third-party tutoring services and other remedial solutions" from current $21.9 billion to "more than $28 billion" by the 2008–2009 school year. Clearly lots of money is to be made by publishers and private agencies off the "failure" of the public schools as promulgated and perpetuated by the same publishers (Kohn, 2004). Apparently those forces have learned the value of vested self-interest.

The greatest hope for a safe, sane, and democratic future lies in public education and those students who have the opportunity to learn more than mere facts.

Throw into the mix the dumbing and dulling down of the curriculum mentioned earlier, and you have a recipe for the undermining and ultimate destruction of public education in America. If that is, in fact, the true goal of the current alliance of business and political forces, then one has to further wonder about the future of democracy in America.

Fortunately, we are seeing some signs of rising dissatisfaction with the realities NCLB's rhetoric has created for public education and our students. So perhaps there is hope that the tide is turning. After all, the greatest hope for a safe, sane, and democratic future lies in public education and those students who have the opportunity to learn more than mere facts. Which brings us back to where we started: the true success of integrative, student-driven programs is their ability to teach the so-called facts while simultaneously providing students with higher-level metacognitive skills and democratic social skills they will need to succeed in their future—and it is *their* future. To equip them for that future with anything less than the very best is tantamount to sending troops into harm's way without the best in arms and armor.

Samantha appreciated the learning and leadership opportunities that Soundings afforded her.

I opened this chapter with a quotation from Jordan E., who was in the very first year of Soundings. I'd like to close with a longer statement written a few weeks ago by his younger sister, Samantha, who was a member of the Soundings VI class. As she was finishing her freshman year at our high school, Samantha volunteered the following message to be conveyed to seventh graders as they decide whether or not to participate in a future Soundings.

Here are some of the things that I now can do because of Soundings.

- *I can now speak in public easily.*
- *I learned how to be more organized.*
- *I learned how to analyze and learn reading material. I actually ask myself questions about the reading, which has become a habit because of Soundings. And I predict and make assumptions on the reading, which is very good for English courses in the high school.*

- *I learned how to manage my time and not wait till the day before a paper is due to actually do it. I can now work bit by bit and get papers and projects accomplished efficiently.*
- *I learned how to research properly and how to write a real research paper.*
- *I learned how to write and actually be good at it, as some would say.*
- *I learned how to think out of the box and make my projects and papers different from others'.*
- *I learned leadership and how to take control in times of need.*

And the main thing I learned how to do was how to learn.

I now know how to teach myself new things and make them stick with me. Some teachers at the high school don't go over a lot of the materials or take the time to discuss them in class, but you'll still have a test or quiz, and that's when I need to teach myself all of the information. In Soundings I learned techniques of mastering my own brain. And the one thing I never do anymore is memorize. Never memorize, always learn. That's the key to success. I learned everything I was taught in Soundings: for example, connotation and denotation, which were guaranteed to be discussed in high school, and sure enough they were. Because I learned that and didn't memorize it and then just forgot it, I was the only person in my class who knew what the definitions were. That's a moment that I knew Soundings worked for me.

When all is said and done, the reality of Soundings proves the validity of its rhetoric— and provides ultimate hope for the future.

Soundings VIII began its educational adventure in September 2006. Before the school year is over, these students, like their predecessors, will acquire real understandings of democracy, our country's history and status, the nature of the physical world, humankind, and themselves. Beyond these essential learnings, they will further develop the social skills and positive dispositions needed to become productive family members and citizens in their democratic society.

References

Alexander, W. M., Carr, D., & McAvoy, K. (1995). *Student-oriented curriculum: Asking the right questions.* Columbus, OH: National Middle School Association.

Beamon, G. W. (2001). *Teaching with adolescent learning in mind.* Arlington Heights, IL: Skylight Professional Development.

Beane, J. A. (1995). *A middle school curriculum: From rhetoric to reality* (2nd ed.). Columbus, OH: National Middle School Association.

Beane, J. A. (2005). *A reason to teach: Creating classrooms of dignity and hope.* Portsmouth, NH: Heinemann.

Borba, M. (1996). *Esteem builders complete program.* Austin, TX: Jalmar Press.

Bradbury, R. (1991). *Fahrenheit 451.* New York: Ballantine Books.

Brazee, E., & Capelluti, J. (1995). *Dissolving boundaries: Toward an integrative curriculum.* Columbus, OH: National Middle School Association.

Burkhardt, R. M. (1994). *The inquiry process: Student-centered learning.* Logan, UT: Perfection Learning.

Dickinson, T. (Ed.) (2001). *Reinventing the middle school.* New York: RoutledgeFalmer.

Dillon, S. (March 26, 2006). Schools cut back subjects to push reading and math. *New York Times.* Retrieved March 29, 2006, from http://www.nytimes.com

Fluegelman, A. (Ed.) (1976). *The new games book.* Garden City, NY: Dolphin Books/Doubleday & Company, Inc.

Fluegelman, A. (Ed.) (1981). *More new games.* Garden City, NY: Dolphin Books/Doubleday & Company, Inc.

Friedman, T. L. (2005). *The world is flat: A brief history of the twenty-first century.* New York: Farrar, Straus and Giroux.

George, P. S., & Lounsbury, J. H. (2000). *Making big schools feel small: Multiage grouping, looping, and schools-within-a-school.* Westerville, OH: National Middle School Association.

Jackson, A. W., & Davis, G. A. (2000). *Turning points 2000: Educating adolescents in the 21st century.* New York: Teachers College Press.

Kohn, A. (2000). *The schools our children deserve.* Boston: Houghton Mifflin.

Kohn, A. (2004). *What does it mean to be well educated?* Boston: Beacon Press.

Lounsbury, J. H. (1992). *As I see it.* Columbus, OH: National Middle School Association.

National Middle School Association. (2003). *This we believe: Successful schools for young adolescents.* Westerville, OH: Author.

Nansel, T. R., Overpeck, M., Pilla, R. S., Ruan, W. J., Simons-Morton, B., & Scheidt, P. (2001). Bullying behaviors among U.S. youth: Prevalence and association with psychosocial adjustment. *The Journal of the American Medical Association, 285* (16), 2094-2100. Retrieved April 15, 2006, from http://jama.ama-assn.org

National Forum to Accelerate Middle-Grades Reform. (2004). *Policy statement on small schools and small learning communities.* Newton, MA. Retrieved October 10, 2006, from http://www.mgforum.org/Policy/small%20communities/small%20communities.pdf

Pate, P. E., Homestead, E., & McGinnis, K. (1997). *Making integrated curriculum work: Teachers, students, and the quest for coherent curriculum.* New York: Teachers College Press.

Rose, R. (1981). Twelve angry men (stage version by Sherman L. Sergel). In L. Grindstaff and R. A. Bennett (Eds.), *Exploring literature* (pp. 382-422). Lexington, MA: Ginn and Company.

Sizer, T. R. (1984). *Horace's compromise: The dilemma of the American high school.* Boston: Houghton-Mifflin.

Sizer, T. R. (1992). *Horace's school: Redesigning the American high school.* Boston: Houghton-Mifflin.

Springer, M. A. (1994). *Watershed: A successful voyage into integrative learning.* Columbus, OH: National Middle School Association.

Toffler, A. (2006, April 1). Futurist Alvin Toffler on the economy of tomorrow: Traps and opportunities. *Bottom Line/Personal,* 7.

White, G. (1996). *Overall impressions of the Radnor Middle School Program—Final report.* Lehigh, PA: The Lehigh University Middle Level Partnership.

Wiggins, G., & McTighe, J. (1999). *Understanding by design.* Alexandria, VA: Association for Supervision and Curriculum Development.

Winerip, M. (2006, March 22). Standardized tests face a crisis over standards. *New York Times.* Retrieved March 29, 2006, from http://www.state.ct.gov

APPENDIX 1

ORIENTATION AND SELECTION DOCUMENTS

The following documents were used to prepare for Soundings VIII, 2006–2007. They represent several small but important changes in the process from the way it had been done previously, as was described in an early chapter of the book. First of all, for the first time there is no longer any weighting bias against former Watershed students. As of this spring, all students have an equal chance of getting into Soundings, regardless of previous participation either in Watershed or in the new sixth grade integrated program, Crossroads.

Another change concerns the timing. We moved the entire selection process from February, which we thought was far too early in the year, to late April. This, of course, necessitated condensing the time line, which had a few repercussions. First, we decided to have a large meeting for all parents to cover all three programs at the same time toward the very end of April. This meeting was widely publicized on our school Web site and on our program Web sites as well. In addition, it was included in our school's monthly newsletter that is mailed home to every student's family. Second, we made it clear that putting one's name into the lottery meant the student and parent were agreeing to participate if selected by the lottery. Finally, the new process called for the integrated class lists to be revealed over the summer, as are the other lists. This meant we would no longer meet with the new class before the summer break. Summer packets would be mailed to them along with their notification of selection in the lottery. The class portrait could not be taken until the first day of school.

The following notice was included with the March and April monthly newsletters that went home to every student's family. Also included was the form that students complete to express their interest and the formal letter of invitation that was subsequently addressed to the parents of those students. Finally, there was a copy of the responsibilities participants were asked to accept.

IMPORTANT INFORMATION REGARDING
THE INTEGRATED PROGRAMS

As you begin to begin to think about your child's next school year, you have some important choices to consider. One of those choices involves Radnor Middle School's three integrated programs—Crossroads in 6th grade, Watershed in 7th, and Soundings in 8th.

Unlike the conventional teams to which students are assigned, participation in these integrated programs is based on student and parent choice. Selection is ultimately determined by a lottery, but only those students and parents who choose to participate will be included in that lottery.

To help you make an informed decision, we try to provide everyone with as much information as possible. This starts with presentations of each program to all the students in fifth, sixth, and seventh grades respectively. These presentations occur during the school day shortly before or after spring break. At these presentations the students will be asked to indicate in a ***non-committal*** way whether or not they are interested in being part of the integrated team next year.

Parents of students who express an interest will then receive a formal invitation to attend an informational meeting scheduled for the evening of <u>Monday, April 24th, 2006</u>.

Parents of students who did not express an interest are also welcome to attend this meeting in case they want to encourage their child to reconsider, but they will not receive a letter.

The informational meeting will start with a general introduction to the philosophy of the integrated learning communities. Separate breakout sessions will follow to describe Crossroads, Watershed, and Soundings specifically, and to answer any questions concerning the individual programs. At these meetings, families will receive a form on which to indicate whether or not they want to have their student's name placed in the selection lottery.

Families will have about five (5) days following the meeting to turn in their forms before the lottery is conducted. **Unlike past years, when they choose to participate in the lottery, students will be committing themselves to participate in the respective program if selected by the lottery.**

If you have any questions about this procedure, please contact your child's guidance counselor or any of the teachers in the integrated programs.

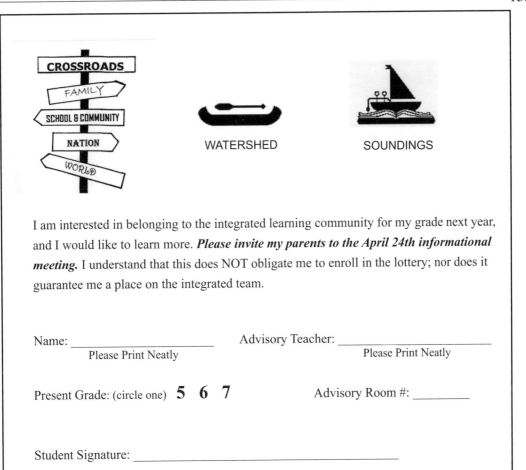

WATERSHED

SOUNDINGS

I am interested in belonging to the integrated learning community for my grade next year, and I would like to learn more. ***Please invite my parents to the April 24th informational meeting.*** I understand that this does NOT obligate me to enroll in the lottery; nor does it guarantee me a place on the integrated team.

Name: _____   Advisory Teacher: _____
        Please Print Neatly   Please Print Neatly

Present Grade: (circle one) **5   6   7**   Advisory Room #: _____

Student Signature: _____

RADNOR MIDDLE SCHOOL   INTEGRATED LEARNING COMMUNITIES

April 2006

Dear Parent(s),

After recently hearing a description of the Radnor Middle School's integrated learning community for his/her next grade, your child has expressed an interest in participating.

Unlike the traditional teams A and B at each grade level to which students are assigned, participation on an integrated team requires both expressed student interest and parental permission. While placement is ultimately determined through a computerized drawing, your child will need your consent to be placed into this lottery.

To help you make an informed decision, we invite you to attend a meeting on the evening of April 24, 2006, here at the middle school. This meeting will start in the auditorium at 7:00 p.m. with a very brief overview of the history and philosophy behind our three integrated programs. Then each team will meet separately with its prospective participant families in different locations to address the specifics of that program and to answer any questions.

At the close of this meeting, families will receive a form on which to indicate their choice to participate or not participate in the lottery. Families will have about five days to make this decision and turn in the form before the lottery is held around May 1st. Please note that by entering the lottery you will be making a commitment to participate in the program if selected by the lottery. Placements for all teams, integrated and traditional, will be announced over the summer.

Given the importance of this decision, we urge you to attend the May 4th meeting. If for any reason you cannot attend this meeting, please contact your child's guidance counselor or one of the teachers in the integrated programs to address any questions you may have and to obtain the lottery participation form.

Thank you for your interest and support, and we look forward to seeing you on May 4th.

Mark A. Springer   William F. Laffey
Teacher: Soundings Program   Principal

SOUNDINGS: PARTICIPANTS' RESPONSIBILITIES

I. STUDENTS: Each student who elects to participate in Soundings will be expected

Generally:

- to produce quality work that is complete and on time
- to look for wider relationships and applications
- to participate actively and positively in all class endeavors
- to take pride in his/her work and progress
- to accept responsibility for his/her behavior and accomplishments
- to strive to go beyond basic stated expectations

Specifically:

- to pay attention and cooperate at all times
- to treat others with respect at all times
- to keep a daily, written log summarizing each day's activities and accomplishments
- to set specific goals for the year, for each week, and for each day
- to take home and share with his/her parents the weekly assessment form
- to complete a minimum of an hour's worth of Soundings homework each evening
- to care properly for materials and equipment involved in our work
- to try new experiences with a positive attitude
- to be responsible for his/her comfort on any trips outside of school
- to be concerned for safety in all situations

II. PARENTS who elect to participate in Soundings will be expected

- to show an active interest in their child's learning experiences
- to support the student's efforts toward fulfilling the responsibilities listed above
- to reinforce those efforts by
  - discussing each day's activities with the student
  - following the progress of specific assignments
  - checking the weekly assessment sheet
  - insisting that the student devote at least an hour each evening to Soundings-related homework
  - to attend whenever possible Soundings activities, e.g., open houses, meetings, conferences, field trips
  - to communicate questions and concerns to the teachers whenever the need arises.

APPENDIX 2

Summer Packet Materials

The following section contains most of the pages of the annual summer packet we give or send to incoming Soundings students to prepare them for the start of their Soundings year. We list materials they will need and provide ways to contact us over the summer should they have questions or concerns. The packet also presents informative and reassuring advice from previous year's class members. The homework assignments are designed to give students a head start on important discussions to come, such as those involving goals and guidelines, as well as the all-important question-generating process. Required reading journal indexes and descriptions are included as well.

Several letters to parents accompany this packet (pp. 174-176). The request for an e-mail address and one for a description of their goals help involve the parents directly in the learning community. A letter about the reading journal urges them to take an active role in monitoring their child's education.

Included are those pages that remain generally the same from year to year. Reading assignments change from year to year, based on the curriculum set by the district. The same is true with the Time Line Assignment, so these items are not included here.

SOUNDINGS

AN INTEGRATIVE PROGRAM FOR EIGHTH GRADERS

June 2006

Dear _____,

Welcome to SOUNDINGS!!

We are pleased that you have decided to be a member of the eighth SOUNDINGS class. This makes you a very special person, and we're looking forward to working with you. Your enthusiasm and your efforts will make this a truly outstanding educational experience for us all. We are very excited about the coming year, and we hope you are, too. After all, this will be your chance to show the world what eighth graders can do!

To help you prepare, we're giving you this packet of materials and information, which we hope you'll find useful. Please read through these materials carefully and complete the various assignments. They are designed to give you a head start on your work so we can get right into our adventures in the autumn. Let us know if you have any questions or problems. Feel free to contact us at school if we can be of any assistance.

Have a safe, happy, and relaxing summer! Let us hear from you!

Mr. Springer   Mrs. Canniff

ENCLOSED: List of materials you will need
Fundamental Responsibilities
Goal Sheet
Asking the Right Questions
Eighth Grade Summer Reading Requirement
Reading Journal Requirements and List of Classics
Important Literary Terms
Topical Reading and Assignment (not included here)
Time Line Assignment (not included here)
Advice From Soundings VI
Some More Summer Activities

Parent Letters: E-mail form, Reading Journal Letter, Goals Form

THINGS YOU WILL NEED FOR SOUNDINGS

At school, we will be involved in a wide variety of activities. Any special or unusual materials will be provided for you. There are, however, a few items you should acquire and <u>have with you in class each day</u>, right from day #1.

- A sturdy three-ring binder (rings at least 2 inches in diameter) with a set of dividers to organize your materials
- An 8.5 X 11-inch spiral notebook, three to five subject, college ruled
- A 100-page Bound Composition Book for your <u>Reading Journal</u>
- A calendar that shows a month on each page, with holes to keep in your binder
- Pencils and pens for writing, and a set of colored pencils (optional) for drawing
- A reading book

You may also find the following items useful to keep handy in your desk: scissors, scotch tape, correction fluid, a stapler, a ruler, a hole punch, a set of markers, page reinforcements, and white glue.

We will provide you with the following:

- A school assignment book
- A log notebook with log sheets for the entire year.

The most important things that you need to bring each day are

YOUR IDEAS
and a
POSITIVE ATTITUDE!

SOUNDINGS

FUNDAMENTAL RESPONSIBILITIES

Though we will be working together to determine the specific direction and design of our studies this coming year, there are certain broad but fundamental responsibilities which you all must fulfill as part of the RMS curriculum. These fundamentals are tied to the district's version of the Pennsylvania State Standards and are thus requirements that each student must satisfy to complete Soundings successfully. Each specified responsibility will eventually have a complete set of rubrics to guide us toward improvement and success. Some of these rubrics are preordained; others we can help delineate. The fundamental responsibilities include:

1. Maintaining a daily log book or journal of learning activities

2. Maintaining a reading journal with a target of 25 entries

3. Completing at least one research project and paper

4. Planning and conducting a student-led conference with parents and teachers

5. Maintaining a portfolio or file of all work, in addition to the district writing portfolio

6. Completing all biweekly assessment documents and the associated sharing procedures

7. Demonstrating the ability to use computer technologies including word processing, Internet research, presentation programs (PowerPoint and Hyper Studio), and distance communications (e-mail)

8. Demonstrating the ability to give effective presentations to various types of audiences

9. Demonstrating familiarity with essential skills and concepts established by the district standards, in particular as they apply to the specific themes we decide to pursue in Soundings.

SOUNDINGS: SETTING GOALS

(note: these pages are decorated with engaging and often humorous graphics)

When we want to travel somewhere we have never been before, we have to select a destination and then use a map to plan a suitable route. The same is true in life and in school, both of which are journeys of a sort. We need to ask ourselves: *Where do we want to go?* —in other words, what do we want to achieve? —and *how can we best get there?*

Answering these questions gives us direction and purpose, and we call this process setting goals and objectives. Successful people decide what they want and then focus on achieving their goals.

In Soundings, your eighth grade experience will be based upon your goals. You will be encouraged to use and to expand ALL of your abilities to reach the goals you set for yourself.

So let's practice. Think about high school and college, or about a career. What might you like to be doing five or ten years from now? What will you need to do or to know in order to get to those points? What are some of your goals for your eighth grade year?

Name: _____

My long-term goals:

1. _____

2. _____

My goals for this year:

1. _____

2. _____

SOUNDINGS: Asking the Right Questions   Name: _____

Topic ideas can lead us in many directions. Questions we ask often determine the outcome of any exploration, but just as often they can lead us to unexpected connections and discoveries. For example, I could start with a simple topic such as "breakfast." Using this topic as a starting point, I could ask many different questions and head off in many different directions; each new question leading to a host of other possibilities.

To continue our example, I could ask: *What do we eat for breakfast?* This is what we call a Factual Question. It has a definite answer or answers, such as "cereal" or "pancakes." I might then ask questions about health, nutrition, energy, or the human body—*What effects do certain foods have on the body? How is energy contained in the food? How is it released? How is it used in the body?* These are all more sophisticated, factual questions, which we could look up, and answer with a high degree of accuracy. Similarly, I might also inquire about cultural connections having to do with what we eat for breakfast —*Does every culture eat "breakfast," or the same foods for breakfast?*

Eventually, if we keep asking factual questions, we reach a point where real thinking sets in and Research Questions arise. Research Questions are the questions for which an answer is not yet known for certain. *Why are some foods associated with breakfast in one culture but not in another? Do cultural beliefs determine what is or is not "breakfast"? How can breakfast choices reflect cultural, ethnic, or religious beliefs? How can breakfast influence a culture's economy? Does breakfast come only at a certain time of the day? How was this decided? How was time, itself, determined? How does time affect cultures.*

The goal here is to look for connections and to see how our questions can lead us to new discoveries. Following a trail of logical questions from the simple and factual can lead to complex research questions and sophisticated inquiry issues. In Soundings, we challenge you to think deeply, to explore connections, and to move beyond the factual questions one normally encounters in middle school.

Try this yourself!

Asking the Right Questions:

1. Write down a topic: _____

2. Now think of a simple question about this topic. (Stuck? Try starting with "What" or "When" or "Where" or "Who" applied to your topic):

3. Now see if you can create a trail of at least seven more questions that arise from the first one:

4. Looking back over your questions, which are definitely Factual Questions, and which do you think are Research Questions?

Soundings: Eighth Grade Summer Reading Assignment

You, along with all eighth graders, are required to read at least two books over the summer. You should have received a list of suggested summer reading books from the eighth grade Language Arts Department. You may select from that list or from the list enclosed here.

After you read your first selection, please enter it into your new Reading Journal (see "Things you will need for Soundings") using the following format:

Title: <u>Book Title Underlined</u>

Author:

Entry #1

   Setting: Describe the time and place in which the story occurs.

   Characters: Describe the main characters in detail. Give brief overviews of other significant, though lesser characters.

   Conflict: Explain the major or central conflict of the book.

   Plot Synopsis: Please summarize the plot. Try to be concise: aim for a single page of summary

   Personal Reaction: Express your own reactions to the book. Try to avoid general terms such as "good," "nice," and "boring." Try to support your opinions with specific reasons or examples from the text.

For your second book, devise a format that you think adequately serves to review the book. Think carefully about possible options. For example, you might write a letter to the author or to a character. You might create a new ending or design a cover that captures the essence of the book. We will be discussing such options as a class and deciding as a group what type or types of formats we want to use for our 25-book journal. Your ideas will be important to this discussion, and your second journal entry will serve as an example.

Of course, these two books will count as your first two entries of the year to start you on your way toward our 25-book goal. If you read additional books over the summer, include them as well, using the Book #1 format shown above. Any additional books do <u>not</u> have to be selected from the reading list.

Enjoy your summer reading!

SOUNDINGS READING JOURNAL

Name: _____   200_ – 200_

Page	Title	Author	Series (if applicable)	Genre	Date of Entry	OK

SOUNDINGS READING JOURNAL

200_ Requirements/Summary   200_

Name:

Requirements:

     Twenty-five (25) entries
     (must be of suitably challenging quality)
     Complete and accurate index including:
     journal page #, title, author, genre, series
     (if applicable), date of entry
     At least four books by same author
     At least five different authors
     At least four different genres
     (Mystery, Science Fiction, Historical Fiction,
     Western, Contemporary, Fantasy, Drama,
     Non-Fiction, Biography, Autobiography)
     At least three "classics"
     At least two public documents
     Complete and accurate summary page

All entries concerning works of Fiction MUST
adequately describe:

     Title and author
     Setting: time and place
     Characters: (important traits and relationships)
     Plot and conflict
     Critical assessment

All entries concerning works of Non-Fiction MUST
adequately describe:

     Title and author
     Topic, theme, main idea or thesis
     Key information /Supporting details presented
     Critical assessment

_____ Reading Journal

Summary:

Genres Represented: Title and Author

Drama _____

Fantasy _____

Historical Fiction _____

Mystery _____

Contemporary _____

Science Fiction _____

Western _____

Non-Fiction _____

Autobiography _____

Biography _____

Books by Same Author: Author:

1. _____ 2. _____

3. _____ 4. _____

Classics I read:

1. _____ 2. _____

3. _____

Public Documents I read:

1. _____ 2. _____

Five different authors I read this year:

1. _____ 2. _____

3. _____ 4. _____

5. _____

SOUNDINGS

Some Classic Works to Consider

* indicates selection is a drama/play

Alcott, Louisa May	Little Women
Angelou, Maya	I Know Why the Caged Bird Sings
Armstrong, William	Sounder
Baldwin, James	Go Tell It on the Mountain
Borland, Hal	When the Legends Die
Bradbury, Ray	Fahrenheit 451
	The Martian Chronicles
Bronte, Charlotte	Jane Eyre
Bronte, Emily	Wuthering Heights
Buck, Pearl	The Good Earth
Carroll, Lewis	Alice in Wonderland
Cervantes, Miguel de	The Adventures of Don Quixote de la Mancha
Clarke, Arthur C.	Childhood's End
	2001: A Space Odyssey
Cooper, James Fennimore	The Last of the Mohicans
Cormier, Robert	I am the Cheese
	The Chocolate War
Crane, Stephen	The Red Badge of Courage
Craven, Margaret	I Heard the Owl Call My Name
Defoe, Daniel	Robinson Crusoe
Dickens, Charles	A Christmas Carol
	A Tale of Two Cities
	David Copperfield
	Great Expectations
	Oliver Twist
Doyle, Arthur Conan	Sherlock Holmes: The Complete Novels and Stories
Dumas, Alexandre	The Count of Monte Cristo
	The Three Musketeers
Eliot, George	Silas Marner

Fitzgerald, F. Scott	The Great Gatsby
Frank, Anne	The Diary of a Young Girl
Gaines, Ernest J.	The Autobiography of Miss Jane Pittman
Golding, William	Lord of the Flies
Hailey, Alex	Roots
Hansberry, Lorraine	Raisin in the Sun*
Hawthorne, Nathanial	The House of Seven Gables
	The Scarlet Letter
Heller, Joseph	Catch 22
Hemingway, Ernest	A Farewell to Arms
	For Whom the Bell Tolls
	The Old Man and the Sea
	The Sun Also Rises
Hesse, Hermann	Siddhartha
Hinton, S.E.	The Outsiders
Hugo, Victor	The Hunchback of Notre Dame
	Les Miserables
Huxley, Aldous	Brave New World
Joyce, James	A Portrait of the Artist as a Young Man
Keyes, Daniel	Flowers for Algernon
Kipling, Rudyard	Captains Courageous
Knowles, John	A Separate Peace
Lawrence, Jerome & Robert Lee	Inherit the Wind*
Lee, Harper	To Kill a Mockingbird
London, Jack	Call of the Wild
	Sea Wolf
	White Fang
Miller, Arthur	Death of a Salesman*
	The Crucible*
Morrison, Toni	Beloved
	The Bluest Eye

Orwell, George	Animal Farm	Swift, Jonathan	Gulliver's Travels
	1984	Thoreau, Henry David	Walden
Paton, Alan	Cry the Beloved Country	Tolkien, J.R.R.	The Hobbit
Peck, Robert Newton	A Day No Pigs Would Die		The Lord of the Rings
Poe, Edgar Allan	The Complete Tales and Poems of E. A. Poe	Twain, Mark	The Adventures of Tom Sawyer
			The Adventures of Huckleberry Finn
Potok, Chaim	The Chosen		A Connecticut Yankee in King Arthur's Court
Rawlings, Marjorie Kinnan	The Yearling		
Richter, Conrad	The Light in the Forest		The Prince and the Pauper
Rose, Reginald	Twelve Angry Men*		
Salinger, J.D.	Catcher in the Rye	Verne, Jules	Around the World in Eighty Days
Saroyan, William	The Human Comedy		
Shakespeare, William	Romeo and Juliet*		Journey to the Center of the Earth
	Julius Caesar*		
	A Midsummer Night's Dream*		Twenty Thousand Leagues Beneath the Sea
	The Taming of the Shrew*		
	King Lear*	Vonnegut, Kurt	Slaughterhouse Five
Shaw, George Bernard	Pygmalion*		Cat's Cradle
Shelley, Mary	Frankenstein	White, T.H.	The Once and Future King
Speare, Elizabeth	The Witch of Blackbird Pond		
		Wilder, Thornton	Our Town*
Steinbeck, John	Of Mice and Men	Williams, Tennessee	The Glass Menagerie*
	The Pearl	Wyss, Johann	The Swiss Family Robinson
	The Red Pony		
Stevenson, Robert Louis	Dr. Jekyll and Mr. Hyde	Zindel, Paul	The Pigman
	Kidnapped		
	Treasure Island		
	The Black Arrow		

Soundings   **Important Literary Terms**

Name: _____

I. From the list of literary terms select the term that fits each definition and write it on the space provided.

The Literary Terms

Abstract Language	Alliteration	Allusion	Apostrophe
Assonance	Concrete Language	Connotation	Consonance
Denotation	Figurative Language	Hyperbole	Literal Language
Metaphor	Meter	Metonymy	Onomatopoeia
Personification	Simile	Symbol	Synecdoche

1. _____ a direct comparison using "like" or "as."
2. _____ language that expresses particular, specific objects.
3. _____ addressing an absent person or object as if it were present.
4. _____ the use of a word to represent or imitate a sound.
5. _____ a pattern of stressed and unstressed syllables.
6. _____ a person, object, action, or situation used to represent something else.
7. _____ a reference to another work of literature.
8. _____ repetition of the first letter or sound in two or more words in the same line.
9. _____ an implied comparison between two unlike things.
10. _____ language that says exactly what it means.
11. _____ the specific, dictionary definition of a word.
12. _____ using part of a thing to represent the entire thing.
13. _____ language that expresses ideas or generalities, usually in representative terms.
14. _____ giving human characteristics to non-human things.
15. _____ poetic language using techniques such as metaphor, simile, and synecdoche.
16. _____ the general and/or emotional, implied associations carried by a word.
17. _____ the substitution of an object for an idea closely associated with it.
18. _____ repetition of vowel sounds in a line or sentence.
19. _____ intentional exaggeration for effect.
20. _____ repetition of consonant sounds in a line or sentence.

II. Now let's see how many figures of speech you can recognize. On the space
provided, write the term that best labels each example:

Alliteration   Apostrophe   Hyperbole   Metaphor

Metonymy   Personification   Simile   Synecdoche

1. _____   "All the world's a stage."

2. _____   "The White House announced today ..."

3. _____   "She sells seashells by the seashore."

4. _____   "The wind whispered to the trees. . ."

5. _____   "Death, be not proud . . ."

6. _____   "All hands on deck!"

7. _____   "The dawn came up like thunder . . ."

8. _____   "Mr. Springer is older than the hills!"

III. Can you write some of your own? Select three of the figures of speech used above
and create your own example for each. (Feel free to try others on a separate sheet and
attach them if you would like.)

<u>Figure of Speech:</u>   <u>Example:</u>

1._____: _____

2._____: _____

3._____: _____

Advice from Soundings VI

"Listen to what my classmates and I have to say to you. You are welcome to read and take advantage of this advice [we are] about to give you, or you can flip through the rest of the packet and pretend to be reading it. Whatever decision you choose will almost certainly indicate the kind of student you will be for your Soundings year." C.J.

"Get ready to dive in, because you are about to explore all the layers and depths of Soundings. That's what Soundings is about, exploring new things, taking risks, and developing a greater awareness of yourself and your surroundings. Soundings is a unique experience, one you may only have once in your life. With any new experience there is usually a sense of uncertainty, and you may feel overwhelmed. I promise you these feelings will cease. Since you interact with the same people most of the day, Soundings will begin to feel like a community, a close-knit family. It will begin to feel comforting, reassuring, a place where you belong." A.H.

"If you want to accomplish great things, you have to set great goals. Goals are going to get you farther, in Soundings and in life. When you set goals, dream big; you never know what you can accomplish. Like the famous quote by Anatole France says, 'To accomplish great things, we must dream as well as act.'" M.E.

"In this program you do a lot, and the work might seem overwhelming at times; but I'm here to tell you that you can get through it and have a great year . . . The first thing is never feel you're alone when it comes to a project, and always remember that Mr. Springer and Mrs. Canniff are there to help you when you don't understand something. Also, always keep a positive attitude on all the work that needs to be done because, when you do, the work gets done a lot faster. . . This is going to be a great experience, and in the end you will have learned a great deal . . ." J.J.

"Integrated describes Soundings in many ways . . . Integrated also directly relates to how everyone interacts with each other. The entire year is basically a large group project. Then within this are a large number of smaller group projects. All this teamwork brings the whole class together and creates a fellowship. All the positive thinking that erupts really lightens the spirit of the class as a whole and allows better brainstorming and collaboration. Just contribute to your fullest extent, and help and encourage others to bring their special gifts to the group." P.V.

"Being a student in the Soundings Program gives you a variety of resources, and I advise you to use them. You should take advantage of [the teachers], take advantage of the ability to hand papers in to be edited again and again, take advantage of their ability to help you one-on-one; and most importantly, do not be afraid to try something you never did before or to do more than they tell you to do." B. S.

"This upcoming year can be your most memorable and interesting year of your school career. The Soundings curriculum is completely student-based, meaning that if you have an interest in something, you can incorporate it into your assigned projects... Although this sounds fun, there's work involved. Keep up to date with your assignments." M.M.

"Try to read a variety of genres and reading levels. Reading books like *Of Mice and Men* and *Swiss Family Robinson* can be fun and look good on your record. When you validate a book, you have a variety of choices. You can do a regular entry (snore) or a fun mobile or diorama. When you select topics for your Soundings year, be creative. Whatever comes to mind, say it. Nobody is here to judge you. Choose topics that interest you and you think would be fun to study. Remember that even if you don't get your choice, you can always find a way to incorporate it into your studies." F.W.

"I really enjoyed my year in Soundings and will miss the experience of it. Not only do you get to meet some very interesting people, you can learn anything you want and as deep as you want. Cherish every moment in Soundings because it goes by fast." S.Z.

"A concept I wish I would have realized at the beginning of the school year involves asking for help when you need it. [The Teachers] will be willing to help you if you ask. I asked for help on a density lab, and [teacher] walked me through it so I could turn it in. However, don't believe that they will do your paper for you if you ask them to; they won't; but they will give you pointers on how to construct the paper... So don't ever be afraid to ask for help if you need it." C.S.

"You will have a lot of things to do, whether it is researching, building a project, or just filling in your logbook. Having so many things to do at one time, you need to learn to manage your time. You don't want to be one of those people who sits in class and just reads, or talks the whole time, because this isn't a year off. This is one of the hardest years of your middle school career." S.E.

"During group projects, everybody should do his or her part of the work for a couple of reasons. First of all, the teachers know who does their work and who doesn't; they know everything (dun, dun, dun). Second, your peers in your group will never want to work with you ever again [if you don't do your share of the work]. Last of all, the more you work, the more you will get out of the experience, whether it be more knowledge or more friendships!" D.K.

"This program is a chance to prove to all your other crazy past teachers, and more importantly to yourself, that you are not a failure and can succeed on your own. My advice for you would be to get involved in all the projects. This will first give you a chance to show your classmates what you are made of. Second it will teach you more than you could have ever possibly learned by just sitting there and watching others do the work." H.R.

"Group work is one of my favorite parts of Soundings. During group work, you have a good chance to interact with your friends, get work done, and have fun. You selected your projects, so you should be happy; and if you aren't, it's your own fault for not speaking up."
M.C.

Soundings: Some More Summer "Assignments"

1. Sometime during the summer, from somewhere on your travels—whether to camp, on vacation, or just around Wayne—<u>send us a postcard</u> telling us how your summer is going and what you're doing to have fun. We'd really love to hear from you!! Plus, we'll post all of the cards in our new room so we can all enjoy them when you return in September.

Mail the postcard to: Mr. Springer and Mrs. Canniff
           SOUNDINGS: Radnor Middle School
           131 South Wayne Avenue
           Wayne, PA 19087

You can also email us at   Mark.Springer@rtsd. org

           Mary.Canniff@rtsd.org

2. If you travel over the summer and visit interesting places, try to bring back any brochures or pamphlets. You never know when they might prove useful in our research—and they'll give you a chance to share your experiences with the rest of us!!

We hope you have some fun with all of these short tasks, and that you learn something from each of them. Enjoy your summer and come back ready to make 200_–200_ a great year!

SOUNDINGS

An Integrative Alternative for Eighth Graders

Radnor Middle School
131 South Wayne Avenue
Wayne, PA 19087

June 200_

Dear New SOUNDINGS Parents,

In the continuing effort to improve communication among teachers, parents and students, Mary and I would like to open possibilities for e-mail correspondence with each of you. To this end, here are our e-mail addresses here at school. We check our e-mail every day during the school year, so please feel free to contact us via email at any time.

Mark.Springer@rtsd.org   Mary.Canniff@rtsd.org

We would also appreciate the opportunity to send you notices and information through e-mail if possible. Please complete and return the bottom portion of this form to indicate your preference and to help us confirm that you received this notice. Thank you.

Mark   Mary

_____

Student Name: _____

Please check the appropriate response below. Then please sign this form and return it to us as soon as possible.

_____ I/We prefer NOT to use e-mail communication.

_____ I/We wish to take advantage of e-mail communications. Please use the e-mail address below:

Parent Name:_____   e-mail address: _____

Signature: _____

Parent Name: _____   e-mail address: _____

Signature: _____

Date: _____ 200_

SOUNDINGS

An Integrative Alternative for Eighth Graders

Radnor Middle School
131 South Wayne Avenue
Wayne, PA 19087

June 200_

Dear New SOUNDINGS Parents,

As we hope you have noticed, your child has been asked to think carefully about his/her goals for the coming year and to write down some ideas as one of the Summer Packet assignments. Since you are equal partners in this endeavor, we would also like to know about your thoughts. We ask that you please take a few moments and jot down any goals you have for your child's Soundings experience and any information you think could help us as we strive to meet those goals.

You can return this form to the school over the summer, or you can have your child turn it in the opening day.

Either way, we look forward to hearing from you and to working with you to make your child's Soundings experience the best it can be.

Thank you.

Mark Springer   Mary Canniff

_____

Student's Name: _____

Parent Name(s):_____

My/Our goals for our child in Soundings are:

Parent Signature: _____

SOUNDINGS

An Integrative Alternative for Eighth Graders

Radnor Middle School
131 South Wayne Avenue
Wayne, PA 19087

Dear SOUNDINGS Parents,

The Reading Journal has always been a big part of the Soundings experience, and is now a part of the district's curriculum standards as well. Your child will be asked to try to read at least 25 book or book equivalent texts this year, and to record his or her responses to those readings. Please look over the reading journal guidelines included in this summer packet so you have an understanding of the general expectations involved.

In addition to the journal requirements and indexes, you will also find a list of over 100 books. This list has been put together in response to the numerous requests we receive each year from parents looking for reading ideas to suggest to their students. The list is a compilation of many lists from many sources including libraries, language arts curriculum committees, reading specialists' suggested lists, etc. The titles include a wide array of books representing many genres, many reading ability levels, and many issues and topics, as befits the requirements of the reading journal. We recognize that someone could possibly find some of these books objectionable—indeed, any book could be objectionable to someone somewhere. All, however, are recognized as "classics" by different groups. The goal of the list is not to require students to read all these titles, nor is it to require any specific book from the list be read, but rather to provide a reference resource for you and your student to use as you select books to read.

We always have a wide range of readers in Soundings classes. Many students need books at or below an eighth grade reading level; others are ready and able to tackle more advanced readings. This list provides a starting point for all—which is why the list is so long and so varied. While we might recommend some books over others for particular students, it is not our place to tell anyone what he or she may not read. However, just as clearly, we believe that parents should be involved in helping their children make appropriate selections.

Therefore, we encourage you to be an active participant in your child's choice of reading selections this year, in much the same way as you would monitor your child's television or movie viewing. Furthermore, we encourage you to discuss all reading selections with your student to help him or her understand difficult concepts. Finally, we encourage you to feel free to contact us if you have questions about your child's reading selections or reading progress at any time during our year together.

Mark Springer

APPENDIX 3

LIST OF LOG QUESTIONS

Note: The log question is determined and put on the board each morning by one of the teachers. It may point to a concept we will be learning or an activity we will experience during the day; it may set the stage for the next day's work, or it may reflect back upon previous work. The reader will see procedural questions, specific content questions, analytical and evaluative questions. Some have specific answers; many are intentionally open-ended or subject to multiple interpretations to generate discussion. Scanning these actual log questions for an entire year gives one a glimpse into the types of activities, content, and thinking involved in a Soundings year.

SOUNDINGS VI   **LOG QUESTIONS 2004 – 2005**

9/7   When you think about our year ahead, what "big dreams" do you have for Soundings?

9/8   What characteristics and skills do you need to succeed in school?

9/9   How are rights, privileges, and responsibilities related?

9/10   How do *you* define "consensus," and how do you think we can achieve it?

9/13   In what categories or ways can we communicate your progress to your parents?

9/14   What characteristics would a successful self-assessment document have?

9/15   Regardless of the theme(s) we select, what would be some ways we could possibly put our studies and learning to use to improve our world?

9/17   Regardless of the theme(s) we select, what skills will we need to answer our questions?

9/16   In-service day

9/20   What aspect of the Sandy Hill camp experience are you looking forward to the most?

9/21   What was the best part of your Sandy Hill camp experience?

9/22 – 24 8th grade class trip to Sandy Hill on the Chesapeake; no log questions.

9/27   What functions are served by the section of the school you are designing, and how will your design facilitate completion of those functions?

9/28   How do *you* define "research?"

9/29   How do you conduct research?

9/30   What is plagiarism?

10/1   How do you avoid plagiarism?

10/4   If you could make one recommendation to the school architect, what would you suggest that he consider in his plans for the new middle school?

10/5   What characteristics do effective posters have?

10/6   What are the essential or generic parts or aspects of a system?

10/7   What are the major parts of the human brain, and what is the primary function of each?

10/8   What's the most important thing you'd like visitors to learn about your Soundings class?

10/11   Why do we go through the self-assessment process?

10/12   What are your initial impressions of the world of 2407 in *The Cure*?

10/13   What steps will you need to take to finish your video on time?

10/14   What worked well at our first literary coffeehouse, and what should we try to improve upon next time?

10/15	If you were a blood cell, how would you travel through the body? (Describe your path.)
10/18	If you were a molecule of oxygen, how would you travel through the body? (Describe your path.)
10/19	What is the path of food through the digestive system?
10/20	How do wastes exit the cells and the body?
10/21	How does a nerve impulse travel?
10/22	What are the three basic kinds of muscle, and how do they differ?
10/25	How does the endocrine system differ from other systems we have reviewed?
10/26	What are the major functions of the skeletal system?
10/27	Select two systems and then describe how they work together.
10/28	Which system in the human body is the most important? Why?
10/29	What are the three major structural sections of the brain, and what's the function of each?
11/1	Why are neurotransmitters important?
11/2	In-service day
11/3	What is the most important point you learned and want to tell the class about the disease or disability you are researching?
11/4	Why is the Flu such a dangerous virus?
11/5	What is intelligence?
11/8	What is the purpose for our "Limitations Olympics?"
11/9	How did Mrs. T's talk about her Holocaust experiences relate to the novel, *The Cure*?
11/10	After Dr. M's visit, which project do you think you would most like to sponsor with any money raised from the cartridge recycling?
11/11	Why do we have student-led conferences?
11/12	What were the three most important concepts or facts you learned from Dr. H's talk today about psychiatric medicine?
11/15	After today's dress rehearsals, what would you change in your presentation, or suggest others change in theirs?
11/16	(Repeat previous question for the rest of the group presentation rehearsals.)
11/17	What question(s) are you attempting to answer in your Limitation Olympics activity?
11/18	What is your "hypothesis" for your Limitation Olympics activity?
11/19	How did your Big Brain presentation go today? What worked; what didn't?
11/22	What lessons have you learned from building your first unit that you can apply as we begin to plan our second unit?
11/23 – 26	No school: Student-led Conferences followed by Thanksgiving break.
11/29	In preparation for the architect's visit, please list at least two questions you would like to ask him about plans for the new middle school.
11/30	What information or data did you collect from the Limitation Olympic trials today?
12/1	From the data collected thus far, is your hypothesis being proved or disproved? Why?
12/2	What have you learned about yourself and others from the Limitation Olympics?
12/3	Looking back on your notes from our original theme selection, what is the most important question you would like to address in our next unit?
12/6	Based on the architect's presentation last Friday, what elements would you recommend for the new Soundings room?
12/7	With results now all in, how do your personal results in the Limitation Olympics compare with class averages?
12/8	What is "Culture?"

12/9   How does fantasy literature (subject of tomorrow's literary coffeehouse) relate to our study of cultures?

12/10   What do you think are some possible ways one culture can influence another?

12/13   What is the specific "setting" (time and place) of the culture your group is researching?

12/14   What are some ways the geography and climate influenced your target culture?

12/15   How does culture affect *you*?

12/16   When do you need to cite the sources of information you use in your research paper?

12/17   What lessons about culture do we learn from *Ishmael*? (excerpt from D. Quinn novel)

12/20   What do you think are some cultural beliefs that shape our culture?

12/21   How can you tell if a trait or a concept is a cultural value or belief?

12/22   What cultural beliefs helped shape the culture you are examining?

12/23   How do the December holidays reflect contemporary American cultural beliefs?

12/24 – 1/2   Winter break

1/3   What resolutions have you made for the 2005 portion of your Soundings year?

1/4   What features, buildings, etc., would you expect to find in a typical, contemporary American town?

1/5   What do the common features, buildings, etc. tell us about our culture?

1/6   How is the town you are constructing similar to contemporary American towns?

1/7   What do the similarities and differences between contemporary American towns and the towns in the culture you are studying tell us about cultural similarities and differences?

1/10   What features or characteristics do the buildings in your town have in common?

1/11   What was the "Neolithic Revolution," and why was it important?

1/12   What were some advantages and disadvantages of the Neolithic Revolution?

1/13   How has recent research changed the concept of the Neolithic Revolution?

1/14   Why is food such an important aspect of every culture?

1/17   No School: MLK, Jr. Day-One of Service

1/18   What did you learn about the cultures presented today through their food?

1/19   What are some similarities between the cultures presented today through their food?

1/20   What are some differences between the cultures presented today through their food?

1/21   What made certain feast day presentations more effective than others?

1/24   What do you need to do to make your fashion show a success?

1/25   How would you summarize the role(s) of food in culture?

1/26   What do you think clothing can reveal about a culture?

1/27   Which fashion presentations were most effective and why?

1/28   What functions do sports play in a culture?

1/31   How can your model town's blueprint help you determine your materials list?

2/1   How can I avoid procrastination?

2/2   What did today's events and games reveal about the cultures that played them?

2/3   Based on their games, how did the cultures presented today differ from those we learned about yesterday?

2/4   How do the sports we have studied relate to the Super Bowl?

2/7   How did the last games compare or contrast with the previous ones?

2/8   What can we conclude about sports, games, and culture?

2/9   What roles do the arts play in a culture?

2/10   What questions do you have about high school course selection?

2/11   How are art and language related in any given culture?

2/14   How can you make the best use of the two weeks before your town models are due?

2/15   How are all languages similar? What do they have in common?

2/16	How does language reflect or alter our perceptions of the world?
2/17	What are the two most important concepts you want to teach the class about the language of your study culture?
2/18	What effect(s) did your study culture have on other cultures?
2/21	No School: Presidents' Holiday
2/22	What do the specific architectural characteristics of your town tell us about the culture?
2/23	What would be the two most important things you'd like your audience to learn from viewing your model town?
2/24	If you were a guide, what would you point out about your model to visitors?
2/25	What remains to be finished on your model? What will *you* do to ensure completion?
2/28	Snow day
3/1	What did and did not go well with the museum showings today?
3/2	What did today's motivational assembly reveal about cultural beliefs?
3/3	What is the purpose for having a bibliography for your research paper?
3/4	How do you think "superstition" differs from "belief?"
3/7	What advice would you recommend for 7th graders as they make their decision about Soundings for next year?
3/8	What is DNA and how does it relate to the study of genetics?
3/9	How might genetics relate to or affect cultures?
3/10	How does the article we read today illustrate cultural exchange?
3/11	What new information or understanding did you gain from our guest today and the DNA exercise?
3/14	As we prepare to plan unit 3, what lessons have you learned from planning and implementing unit 2?
3/15	What similarities and differences did you detect between Chinese and Japanese music?
3/16	What have you learned from research paper 1 that will help you improve on research paper 2?
3/17	What do you think oceans and outer space have in common?
Spring break	
3/29	What is the difference between an ocean and a sea?
3/30	What are plate tectonics and how do they affect oceans?
3/31	Describe the parts of a wave: crest, trough, amplitude, wavelength, and period.
4/1	Compare and contrast your experiences at the Cloisters Art Museum and at the Rose Center of the NY Museum of Natural History.
4/4	How does an ocean current differ from a wave?
4/5	What is a "gyre," what causes this phenomenon, and why is the North Atlantic gyre so important to us?
4/6	What is "bathymetry," and why is it important to the study of oceans?
4/7	Based on depth, what are the major zones of the oceans?
4/8	What physical factors determine types and numbers of organisms that live in each zone?
4/11	What are the steps in the hydrologic cycle, and why is this cycle so important?
4/12	Why is water's density so significant?
4/13	How are water density and salinity related, and how could you prove this relationship?
4/14	How did density lab #3 confirm or refute our results from lab #2?
4/15	Why do oceans often appear blue? What other colors can oceans be and why?
4/18	Why was Jacques Cousteau important?
4/19	Describe three major inventions or technological advancements that improved undersea exploration. What was the earliest you could find?

4/20	What might be some difficulties associated with undersea exploration?
4/21	Which invention or advancement we have seen do you think is most significant? Why?
4/22	What is the "Littoral Zone?" Why do we know more about it than about other zones?
4/25	Ecologically speaking, what is a community? What communities exist in the ocean?
4/26	What is "upwelling," and why is it important to oceanic communities?
4/27	Why was the discovery of undersea hydrothermal vents so important, and what does it have to do with outer space exploration?
4/28	Why do you think NASA trains astronauts in an undersea habitat?
4/29	How does earth's relationship with the sun affect the oceans?
5/2	Who was Copernicus, and what did he have to do with space exploration?
5/3	What is gravity, and what is its relationship to our solar system?
5/4	How are speed, velocity, and acceleration related but different?
5/5	How could understanding velocity and acceleration help us explore the universe?
5/6	How can understanding ocean waves help us understand what happens in outer space?
5/9	What is the most interesting new fact or concept you learned on our visit to the National Aquarium today?
5/10	Who was Johannes Kepler? Why was his work important to our understanding of space?
5/11	What was the first manmade object in space? When was it, and who put it there?
5/12	Who and when was the first man in space?
5/13	What have been the major U.S. space programs? Put them in chronological order.
5/16	If you were able to do your formal debate again, what would you do differently?
5/17	In-service day
5/18	What is "cosmology?"
5/19	How would you describe the Big Bang theory?
5/20	In general, what pieces of observable information are scientists using to calculate the age of the universe?
5/23	How would "open" and "closed" universes differ? Why do scientists currently think our universe is "flat?"
5/24	What is the basic concept of relativity?
5/25	What did you think of today's high school orientation program? What did you learn?
5/26	Aside from the obvious information to help us understand outer space, how has the space program had an impact on our culture?
5/31	Why do we have/ "make" constellations?
6/1	What have you learned about your own reading skills or abilities this year?
6/2	How do you prepare for a spelling "final exam?"
6/3	List three new concepts you learned from our unit on oceans and space explorations.
6/6	What new questions do you now have about oceans and/or space exploration?
6/7	What skills have you learned or improved upon this year that will help you in high school and beyond?
6/8	What skill do you want to continue to improve next year?
6/9	Which of your accomplishments this year are you most pleased with and/or proud of?

APPENDIX 4

End of Year Self-Assessment

Name:_____   June 2005

<u>Goals and accomplishments:</u>

1. What have you done to accomplish the goals you have set, and how successful have you been in meeting those goals?

2. What accomplishments are you most proud of and why?

3. From what you have experienced, what are your goals for the future?

4. How have your goal-setting skills improved?

5. From what you have learned, what can be carried to the high school?

6. How will you incorporate what you have learned?

Individual Responsibilities   **Log Book**   Name:_____

Check all that apply.

T	S	Exceptional	T	S	Proficient	T	S	Not Yet Proficient	T	S	Experiencing Difficulty
		Always available			Usually available			Sometimes available			Rarely/Never available
		Up-to-date/ no missing entries			Most entries complete			Several entries missing			Entries rarely complete
		Completed on time			Entries usually on time			Entries sometimes on time			Entries rarely on time
		Answers show effort			Most answers show effort			Some entries show effort			Entries rarely show effort
		Neat and well organized			Generally neat			Not neat or not organized			Neither neat nor organized
		Goals relate to Soundings			Most goals relate to Soundings			Goals sometimes relate to Soundings			Goals rarely/never relate to Soundings
		Attainable goals			Most goals attainable			Some goals attainable			Goals rarely attainable
		Always wrote quotes on time			Usually wrote quotes on time			Rarely wrote quotes on time			Never wrote quotes on time
		Thorough quote interpretation			Most quote interpretations show thought			Some quote interpretations show thought			Quote interpretations rarely show thought

Comments:

Individual Responsibilities   **Reading Journal**   Name:_____

Check all that apply.

T S Exceptional	T S Proficient	T S Not Yet Proficient	T S Experiencing Difficulty
Appearance			
Entries are neat, legible, and attractive	Entries are generally neat and/or legible	Entries are somewhat neat or legible	Entries are not neat or legible
Indices complete	Indices generally complete	Indices not complete	No indices present
Creative and personalized	Creative or personalized	Shows little creativity or personalization	No effort to show creativity
Qualities of Entries			
Complete and thorough entries	Complete entries	Some incomplete entries	Most or all entries incomplete
Wide variety of formats	Some variety of format	Entries similar in format	All entries have the same format
Targets established, always met	Targets established	Targets established, not met	No targets established or met
Always turned in on due date	Always within allotted time	Not always in on time	Rarely/never in on time
Qualities of Writing			
Rare writing errors	Few writing errors	Noticeable writing errors	Many writing errors
Always makes corrections as needed	Usually makes corrects as needed	Makes few of the corrections needed	Rarely or never makes corrections
Qualities of Selections			
Wide variety of reading genres	Some variety of genres	Little variety of genres	No variety of genres
Challenging reading level	Some challenging reading levels	At or below reading ability level	Below reading ability level

Comments:

Individual Responsibilities   **Spelling**   Name:_____

Check all that apply.

T S Exceptional	T S Proficient	T S Not Yet Proficient	T S Experiencing Difficulty
Vocabulary			
Knows majority of definitions	Knows many of the definitions	Knows some definitions	Knows few definitions
Completion			
Always completes work	Completes work most of the time	Completes work some of the time	Rarely or never completes work
Work is completed with high quality	Work is completed with some quality	Work is completed with low quality	Work is left incomplete
Work is always in on time	Rarely late in handing in work	Frequently turns work in late	Never turns in work
Assessments			
Prepares all the time	Prepares frequently	Prepares sometimes	Does not prepare
Does well on assessments	Does all right on assessments	Attempts to do well	Does not try very hard on assessments
Participation			
Participates to fullest ability	Participates sometimes in games	Rarely participates in games	Does not try to participate in games

Comments:

Individual Responsibilities   **Bi-Weekly Self-Assessments**   Name:_____

Check all that apply.

T	S	Exceptional	T	S	Proficient	T	S	Not Yet Proficient	T	S	Experiencing Difficulty
		Answered question clearly and effectively			Answered clearly			Answered vaguely			Missed some answers
		Answered the questions thoroughly			Adequately answered the questions			Limited thoughts shown			Left out some answers
		Self-assessments accurately reflect his or her actions			Self-assessments generally reflect his or her actions			Self-assessments vaguely reflect his or her actions			Self-assessments do not reflect his or her actions
		Handed in on time with the parent's signature			Handed in one or two days late			Handed in three or more days after the due date			Missed some self-assessments

Comments:

Individual Responsibilities   **Assignments**

Check all that apply.

T	S	Exceptional	T	S	Proficient	T	S	Not Yet Proficient	T	S	Experiencing Difficulty
		Assignments always turned in			Assignments often turned in			Assignments rarely turned in			Assignments never turned in
		Assignments always on time			Assignments usually on time			Assignments rarely on time			Assignments never on time
		Assignments show thought and hard work			Most assignments show thought and hard work			Assignments rarely show thought and hard work			Assignments show neither thought nor hard work

Comments:

Writing Name:_____

T S Exemplary	T S Proficient	T S Not Yet Proficient	T S Experiencing Difficulty
Overall Development:			
Fluent, richly developed	Moderately fluent, well developed	Limited development	Not developed
Clear awareness of audience and task	Awareness of audience and task	Poor awareness of audience or task	No awareness of audience or task
Distinctive voice	Some evidence of voice	Little evidence of voice	No evidence of voice
Original, insightful, imaginative	Ideas well developed	Repetitive or too general	Inappropriate response
Organization:			
Carefully but subtly organized	Organized; may have minor lapses	Focus unclear or limited	Lacks organization or focus
Devices subordinate to meaning	Meaning may be subordinate to devices	Shifts perspective or lacks closure	
Clear focus	Focused	Resembles free writing	
Content and Support:			
Supporting details are rich and full	Details adequately support focus	Details lack elaboration	Virtually no supporting details
Details are relevant and appropriate to audience and task	Details are generally relevant and appropriate to audience and task	Some details do not support the focus	Irrelevant details
Sentence Structures:			
Sentence variety enhance effect	Some sentence variety	Little sentence variety	No sentence variety
Virtually no errors in structures	Minor errors in structure	Errors in structure may interfere with meaning	Serious structural errors
Successful use of sophisticated patterns	Attempts to use sophisticated patterns	Relies on simple or repetitive patterns	Too brief to assess
Word Selection:			
Rich, effective vocabulary	Acceptable vocabulary	Simplistic vocabulary	Inadequate or inaccurate vocabulary
Fresh, vivid language	Attempts to use vivid language	Limited word choice	Too brief to assess
Correct usage	Generally correct language	Noticeable errors in usage	Numerous errors in usage
Mechanics:			
Few or no mechanical errors with complete complexity	Some mechanical errors that do not interfere with meaning	Noticeable mechanical errors that may interfere with meaning	Serious mechanical errors that do interfere with meaning

Writing continued   Name: _____

How do you think your writing has changed this year?

Any other comments you would like to make about your writing this year, including specific skills you have learned:

Group Work   Name:_____

Check all that apply.

T	S	Exceptional	T	S	Proficient	T	S	Not Yet Proficient	T	S	Experiencing Difficulty
		Always respects others			Respects others most of the time			Respects others sometimes			Rarely respects others
		Always cooperates with others			Cooperates with others most of the time			Cooperates with others sometimes			Rarely cooperates with others
		Always stays on task			Stays on task most of the time			Stays on task sometimes			Is rarely on task
		Always works well with group			Works well with group most of the time			Works well with group sometimes			Rarely works well with group
		Finished product shows thought and is creative			Finished product shows some thought and is somewhat creative			Finished product shows little thought and hardly any creativity			Finished product is incomplete or not turned in
		Projects are always on time			Projects are mostly on time			Projects are sometimes on time			Projects are rarely or never on time
		Puts in all of available effort			Puts in most of available effort			Puts in some effort			Doesn't put in any effort

How have your group work and cooperation improved throughout the year?

Other comments:

Presentation Skills — Speaking/Content

Name:_____

Check all that apply.

T	S	Exceptional	T	S	Proficient	T	S	Not Yet Proficient	T	S	Experiencing Difficulty
		Very organized and informative			Organized and informative			Somewhat organized and informative			Not organized or informative
		Uses accurate and effective vocabulary			Uses accurate and sometimes effective vocabulary			Vocabulary is not always accurate and effective			Vocabulary is inaccurate or ineffective
		Always maintains eye contact and knows presentation			Usually maintains eye contact and usually knows presentation			Sometimes maintains eye contact			Rarely maintains eye contact
		Uses inflection and expression effectively			Uses inflection and expression somewhat effectively			Sometimes uses some inflection or expression			Uses little or no inflection or expression
		Usually projects loudly and clearly			Sometimes projects loudly and clearly			Rarely projects loudly or clearly			Cannot be heard or understood

Comments:

Presentation Skills — Posters and Models

Check all that apply.

T	S	Exceptional	T	S	Proficient	T	S	Not Yet Proficient	T	S	Experiencing Difficulty
		Very attractive and eye-catching			Attractive and eye-catching			Somewhat attractive or eye-catching			Unattractive or distracting
		Always neat, legible, and can be read from a distance			Usually neat, legible, and can be read from a distance			Somewhat neat or legible, and barely can be read from a distance			Illegible or not neat
		Very organized and informative			Organized and informative			Somewhat organized and informative			Never organized or informative
		Uses materials effectively			Uses materials somewhat effectively			Most materials not used effectively			Materials used ineffectively

Comments:

Culture Unit   **Events Rubric**   Name:_____

Check all that apply.

Art Museum

	T	S	Exceptional	T	S	Proficient	T	S	Experiencing Difficulty
Quality			The project was well thought out			The project was planned a moderate amount			Little or no planning apparent in the project
			The finished product was very good			The finished product was acceptable			The finished product was shoddy or incomplete
Accuracy			All information used was thoroughly researched			Most information was researched; some general connections were made			Hardly any information was researched
			Individuals had full knowledge or subject			Individuals had some knowledge of subject			Individuals did not understand subject
Presentation			Presentation was clear and understandable			Presentation was relatively clear			Presentation was uncoordinated and sloppy
			It held the audience's attention			It held the audience's attention most of the time			It did not hold the audience's attention at all

Comments:

Sports Tournament

	T	S	Exceptional	T	S	Proficient	T	S	Experiencing Difficulty
Quality			The project was well thought out			The project was planned a moderate amount			Little or no planning apparent in the project
			The finished product was very good			The finished product was acceptable			The finished product was shoddy or incomplete
Accuracy			All information used was thoroughly researched			Most information was researched; some general connections were made			Hardly any information was researched
			Individuals had full knowledge or subject			Individuals had some knowledge of subject			Individuals did not understand subject
Presentation			Presentation was clear and understandable			Presentation was relatively clear			Presentation was uncoordinated and sloppy
			It held the audience's attention			It held the audience's attention most of the time			It did not hold the audience's attention at all

Comments:

Culture Unit   **Events Rubric**   Name:_____

Check all that apply.

Language Video/Game	T	S	Exceptional	T	S	Proficient	T	S	Experiencing Difficulty
Quality			The project was well thought out			The project was planned a moderate amount			Little or no planning apparent in the project
			The finished product was very good			The finished product was acceptable			The finished product was shoddy or incomplete
Accuracy			All information used was thoroughly researched			Most information was researched; some general connections were made			Hardly any information was researched
			Individuals had full knowledge or subject			Individuals had some knowledge of subject			Individuals did not understand subject
Presentation			Presentation was clear and understandable			Presentation was relatively clear			Presentation was uncoordinated and sloppy
			It held the audience's attention			It held the audience's attention most of the time			It did not hold the audience's attention at all

Comments:

Towns	T	S	Exceptional	T	S	Proficient	T	S	Experiencing Difficulty
Quality			The project was well thought out			The project was planned a moderate amount			Little or no planning apparent in the project
			The finished product was very good			The finished product was acceptable			The finished product was shoddy or incomplete
Accuracy			All information used was thoroughly researched			Most information was researched; some general connections were made			Hardly any information was researched
			Individuals had full knowledge or subject			Individuals had some knowledge of subject			Individuals did not understand subject
Presentation			Presentation was clear and understandable			Presentation was relatively clear			Presentation was uncoordinated and sloppy
			It held the audience's attention			It held the audience's attention most of the time			It did not hold the audience's attention at all

Comments:

Space and Oceans Unit   **Events Rubric**   Name:_____

Check all that apply.

Timeline	T	S	Exceptional	T	S	Proficient	T	S	Experiencing Difficulty
Quality			The project was well thought out			The project was planned a moderate amount			Little or no planning apparent in the project
			The finished product was very good			The finished product was acceptable			The finished product was shoddy or incomplete
Accuracy			All information used was thoroughly researched			Most information was researched; some general connections were made			Hardly any information was researched
			Individuals had full knowledge or subject			Individuals had some knowledge of subject			Individuals did not understand subject
Presentation			Presentation was clear and understandable			Presentation was relatively clear			Presentation was uncoordinated and sloppy
			It held the audience's attention			It held the audience's attention most of the time			It did not hold the audience's attention at all

Comments:

Debate	T	S	Exceptional	T	S	Proficient	T	S	Experiencing Difficulty
Quality			The project was well thought out			The project was planned a moderate amount			Little or no planning apparent in the project
			The finished product was very good			The finished product was acceptable			The finished product was shoddy or incomplete
Accuracy			All information used was thoroughly researched			Most information was researched; some general connections were made			Hardly any information was researched
			Individuals had full knowledge or subject			Individuals had some knowledge of subject			Individuals did not understand subject
Presentation			Presentation was clear and understandable			Presentation was relatively clear			Presentation was uncoordinated and sloppy
			It held the audience's attention			It held the audience's attention most of the time			It did not hold the audience's attention at all

Comments:

Space and Oceans Unit   **Events Rubric**   Name:_____

Check all that apply.

Space booklet	T	S	Exceptional	T	S	Proficient	T	S	Experiencing Difficulty
Quality			The project was well thought out			The project was planned a moderate amount			Little or no planning apparent in the project
			The finished product was very good			The finished product was acceptable			The finished product was shoddy or incomplete
Accuracy			All information used was thoroughly researched			Most information was researched; some general connections were made			Hardly any information was researched
			Individuals had full knowledge or subject			Individuals had some knowledge of subject			Individuals did not understand subject
Presentation			Presentation was clear and understandable			Presentation was relatively clear			Presentation was uncoordinated and sloppy
			It held the audience's attention			It held the audience's attention most of the time			It did not hold the audience's attention at all

Comments:

Ocean booklet	T	S	Exceptional	T	S	Proficient	T	S	Experiencing Difficulty
Quality			The project was well thought out			The project was planned a moderate amount			Little or no planning apparent in the project
			The finished product was very good			The finished product was acceptable			The finished product was shoddy or incomplete
Accuracy			All information used was thoroughly researched			Most information was researched; some general connections were made			Hardly any information was researched
			Individuals had full knowledge or subject			Individuals had some knowledge of subject			Individuals did not understand subject
Presentation			Presentation was clear and understandable			Presentation was relatively clear			Presentation was uncoordinated and sloppy
			It held the audience's attention			It held the audience's attention most of the time			It did not hold the audience's attention at all

Comments:

Space and Oceans Unit   **Events Rubric**   Name:_____

Check all that apply.

Space Mural	T	S	Exceptional	T	S	Proficient	T	S	Experiencing Difficulty
Quality			The project was well thought out			The project was planned a moderate amount			Little or no planning apparent in the project
			The finished product was very good			The finished product was acceptable			The finished product was shoddy or incomplete
Accuracy			All information used was thoroughly researched			Most information was researched; some general connections were made			Hardly any information was researched
			Individuals had full knowledge or subject			Individuals had some knowledge of subject			Individuals did not understand subject
Presentation			Presentation was clear and understandable			Presentation was relatively clear			Presentation was uncoordinated and sloppy
			It held the audience's attention			It held the audience's attention most of the time			It did not hold the audience's attention at all

Comments:

Ocean Mural	T	S	Exceptional	T	S	Proficient	T	S	Experiencing Difficulty
Quality			The project was well thought out			The project was planned a moderate amount			Little or no planning apparent in the project
			The finished product was very good			The finished product was acceptable			The finished product was shoddy or incomplete
Accuracy			All information used was thoroughly researched			Most information was researched; some general connections were made			Hardly any information was researched
			Individuals had full knowledge or subject			Individuals had some knowledge of subject			Individuals did not understand subject
Presentation			Presentation was clear and understandable			Presentation was relatively clear			Presentation was uncoordinated and sloppy
			It held the audience's attention			It held the audience's attention most of the time			It did not hold the audience's attention at all

Comments:

Space and Oceans Unit   **Events Rubric**   Name:_____

Check all that apply.

Space Model	T	S	Exceptional	T	S	Proficient	T	S	Experiencing Difficulty
Quality			The project was well thought out			The project was planned a moderate amount			Little or no planning apparent in the project
			The finished product was very good			The finished product was acceptable			The finished product was shoddy or incomplete
Accuracy			All information used was thoroughly researched			Most information was researched; some general connections were made			Hardly any information was researched
			Individuals had full knowledge or subject			Individuals had some knowledge of subject			Individuals did not understand subject
Presentation			Presentation was clear and understandable			Presentation was relatively clear			Presentation was uncoordinated and sloppy
			It held the audience's attention			It held the audience's attention most of the time			It did not hold the audience's attention at all

Comments:

Ocean Model	T	S	Exceptional	T	S	Proficient	T	S	Experiencing Difficulty
Quality			The project was well thought out			The project was planned a moderate amount			Little or no planning apparent in the project
			The finished product was very good			The finished product was acceptable			The finished product was shoddy or incomplete
Accuracy			All information used was thoroughly researched			Most information was researched; some general connections were made			Hardly any information was researched
			Individuals had full knowledge or subject			Individuals had some knowledge of subject			Individuals did not understand subject
Presentation			Presentation was clear and understandable			Presentation was relatively clear			Presentation was uncoordinated and sloppy
			It held the audience's attention			It held the audience's attention most of the time			It did not hold the audience's attention at all

Comments:

APPENDIX 5

Sample Standards Addressed, Soundings I

KNOWLEDGE/CONTENT, APPLICATION, and STUDENT PERFORMANCE SKILLS

Based on <u>New Standards</u> and <u>Content Knowledge</u>

(In use at that time: since merged with district standards to align with Pennsylvania state standards)

KNOWLEDGE/CONTENT

I. Reading Skills

1. **general reading process**
   a. generates questions while reading
   b. reflects on what has been learned while reading
   c. identifies rhetorical and literary devices employed
   d. uses specific strategies to clear up confusing parts
   e. summarizes and generalizes
   f. understands materials from the perspectives of the time period in which they were written
   g. identifies author's purpose and point of view

2. **reading literature**
   a. identifies questions of personal significance and seeks to answer them through reading works of literature
   b. identifies specific interests and the literature that will satisfy those interests
   c. identifies main and subordinate characters
   d. compares and contrasts events and characters in literature with events and people in one's own life
   e. understands extended passages of dialogue
   f. recognizes literary devices and elements of plot

3. **reading information**
   a. reads for a variety of purposes: answer a question, form an opinion, skim for facts
   b. identifies main ideas and supporting details

    c. identifies implied as well as stated ideas

    d. recognizes new information and how it can be used

    e. understands technical terms used in informational text

    f. uses the various parts of a text (index, glossary, etc.) to locate specific information

4. reading specific types of literary texts

    a. reads and applies general reading processes to: myths, mysteries, science fiction, historical fiction, realistic fiction, humorous pieces, biographies, and autobiographies

    b. understands the defining features and structure of: myths, mysteries, science fiction, historical fiction, realistic fiction, humorous pieces, biographies, and autobiographies

    c. reads and applies general reading processes to works of poetry

    d. understands the defining features and structure of poetry

    e. reads and applies general reading processes to letters and diaries

    f. understands the defining features and structure of letters and diaries

5. reading specific types of informational texts

    a. reads and applies general reading processes to works about: social studies, geography, science, health, and nutrition.

    b. understands the defining features and structure of works about: social studies, geography, science, health, and nutrition.

    c. reads and applies general reading processes to historical documents, editorials, and news stories

    d. understands the defining features and structure of historical documents, editorials, and news stories

6. using diverse sources to gather information [cf. I.4]

    a. analyzes and interprets political cartoons

    b. reads and applies general reading processes to directions, recipes, tables, and catalogues

II. Writing Skills

1. general writing process

    a. drafts, revises, edits, proofreads

    b. writes for different audiences

    c. writes effective expository essays including ones that present information, show cause and effect relationships, delineate a problem and its possible solution, and describe autobiographical or biographical incidents

d. writes effective persuasive essays

e. writes effective narrative accounts

f. uses proper footnote and bibliography formats

2. style and rhetoric

a. uses descriptive language to clarify and enhance ideas

b. employs transitional devices

c. varies sentence structures according to audience, purpose, and stylistic goals

d. makes effective use of technical terms and notations in writing when and where appropriate

3. grammar and mechanics

a. understands and uses correctly all types of pronouns, adjectives, adverbs, nouns, verbs and conjunctions

b. understands and uses rules for correct spelling

c. understands and uses rules for proper capitalization

d. understands and uses appropriate forms of punctuation.

e. understands and avoids common usage errors

4. information gathering [cf. II.6]

a. interviewing

b. surveying

c. note taking

d. analyzing and organizing components of research topics

e. organizing information

f. using library resources: card catalog, *Reader's Guide to Periodic Literature*, computer catalog

g . uses a variety of resources: newspapers, magazines, internet, dictionaries, encyclopedia, atlases, journals, schedules, software

h. uses primary resources effectively

i. uses multi-media as a way to collect data

III. Listening Skills

1. pays active attention

2. asks clarifying questions

3. takes summary notes

IV. Speaking Skills
1. **planning and organizing**
2. **presentational techniques (eye contact, voice projection, body language)**

V. Language Skills
1. **understands factors that affect use of language**
2. **analyzes language used by others**

VI. Literature Skills
1. **recognizes characteristics of classic literature**
2. **is familiar with examples of classic works, authors, and genres**

VII. Science Skills

1. **understands Physical Science concepts such as:**
   a. properties in matter, chemical reactivity, conservation of matter
   b. motion and forces
   c. transfer of energy

2. **understands Life Science concepts such as:**
   a. structure and function in living systems [cells to ecosystems]
   b. reproduction, heredity, and the role of genes and environment on trait expression
   c. regulation, behavior, and response to environmental stimuli
   d. populations, ecosystems, and the effects of resources and energy transfer on populations

3. **understands Earth and Space Science concepts such as:**
   a. structure of the earth, natural cycles, oceans, weather and climate
   b. Earth's history
   c. Earth's relation to the Solar System
   d. natural resources management

4. **understands Scientific Connections and Applications such as:**
   a. big ideas and unifying concepts
   b. the designed world: e.g. technology and agricultural techniques
   c. health and safety
   d. impact of technology: advantages and disadvantages
   e. impact of science: interactions between science and society

VIII. Social Studies Skills (unavailable at that time)

IX. Thinking Skills

1. **demonstrates Critical Thinking such as:**
   a. Comprehension
   b. Application
   c. Analysis
   d. Synthesis
   e. Evaluation

2. **demonstrates Problem Solving Skills such as:**
   a. understands how systems function
   b. identifies specific problems
   c. considers strategies and implements methods
   d. considers, selects and uses appropriate resources
   e. draws conclusions
   f. shares results
   g. evaluates process and product

3. **demonstrates Scientific Thinking such as:**
   a. experimental design
   b. application of concepts to explain observations and phenomena
   c. using evidence to develop descriptions, explanations and models
   d. recognizing alternative explanations; distinguishing fact from opinion
   e. identifying problems; proposing and implementing solutions, and evaluating the outcomes
   f. working both individually and in teams

4. **demonstrates Creative Thinking such as:**
   a. imagination
   b. forethought
   c. visualization

X. Organizational Skills
1. **demonstrates Materials Management Skills**
2. **demonstrates Time Management Skills**
3. **employs Process/Project Management Techniques**
4. **uses Appropriate Study Skills**

XI. Personal/Social Skills

1. understands and maintains Personal Wellness
   a. self-respect
   b. self-control
   c. physical and emotional health
   d. punctuality
   e. initiative
   f. commitment
   g. pride

2. understands and strives for Social Wellness
   a. respects others
   b. volunteers
   c. cooperates
   d. accepts responsibility
   e. participates constructively in group activities
   f. follows directions

XII. Technology Skills

1. demonstrates competence with Computers
   a. word processing skills
   b. spreadsheet skills
   c. draw program skills
   d. photo program skills
   e. hyperstudio skills
   f. Internet

2. demonstrate competence with other technologies
   a. CD drive
   b. scanner
   c. video recorder
   d. video editing system
   e.. audio recording system
   f. SLR camera
   g. digital camera

APPLICATION SKILLS

Based on New Standards and Knowledge /Content Skills

I. Reading Skills: The student will apply the listed reading skills to:
1. read at least twenty-five (25) books during the year
2. read at least four books on a specific topic or issue, or by a single author
3. read informational materials representing a range of academic disciplines
4. read a variety of public documents

II. Writing Skills: The student will apply the listed writing skills to produce:
1. a report
2. a response to literature
3. a narrative account

Within these productions, the student will demonstrate:
4. an understanding of the rules of the English language
5. an understanding of the writing process including the ability to edit and revise

The student will also:
6. conduct formal written correspondence with a person or an organization beyond the school
7. publish information using several methods and formats

III. Listening Skills: The student will:
1. participate in one-to-one conferences with adults
2. participate in group meetings
3. listen and respond to presentations by others

IV. Speaking Skills: The student will:
1. prepare and deliver an individual presentation

V. Language Skills: The student will:
1. analyze his/her own use of language
2. analyze language used by others

VI. Literature Skills: The student will:
1. respond to non-fiction, fiction, poetry, and drama
2. produce a work in at least one literary genre

VII. Science Skills

1. The student will demonstrate competence with tools and technologies of science by using them to
   a. observe and measure objects, organisms or phenomena
   b. record, store and retrieve data
   c. collect and analyze data
   d. acquire information from multiple sources
   e. recognize sources of bias in data

2. The student will demonstrate effective scientific communication by
   a. representing data in multiple ways
   b. arguing from evidence
   c. critiquing published materials
   d. explaining scientific concepts or procedures to other students
   e. matching form and content to purpose and audience.

3. The student will demonstrate scientific competence by completing at least one major investigation involving all of the following components:
   a. a controlled experiment
   b. field research
   c. design (such as building a model or apparatus)
   d. secondary research

VIII. Social Studies Skills

IX. Thinking Skills
1. Critical Thinking: The student will:
   a. describe, explain, restate or summarize information gathered
   b. apply information gathered to solve problems and produce results
   c. compare and contrast, form generalizations, and draw conclusions based on information examined
   d. use information gathered to design, organize, produce and present appropriate end products
   e. critique and evaluate his/her own work as well as that of others

2. Problem Solving: The student will
   a. design a product
   b. improve a system
   c. plan and organize an event

3. Scientific thinking: The student will:
   a. design and implement experimental techniques and strategies
   b. explain observations and phenomena using scientific concepts
   c. develop descriptions, explanations and models
   d. present alternative explanations; distinguishing fact from opinion
   e. identify problems; propose and implement solutions, and evaluate the outcomes
   f. work effectively both individually and in teams

4. Creative Thinking: The student will:
   a. present ideas through different media
   b. express concepts graphically as well as verbally
   c. contribute original ideas
   d. create products, including stories, that embody aesthetic qualities
   e. predict possible future situations, conditions or outcomes

X. Organizational Skills: The student will
  1. set goals for learning
  2. develop and maintain a schedule
    a. for personal responsibilities
    b. for group project responsibilities

  3. keep his/her materials and work space neat and functional
  4. maintain a record of accomplishments and progress

XI. Personal/Social Skills: The student will:
  1. behave in ways conducive to learning
    a. demonstrate self-control
    b. be punctual to class and with assignments
    c. take pride in his/her own work
  2. act in accordance with commonly accepted rules for safety and health
  3. fulfill personal responsibilities and commitments
  4. assume leadership roles
  5. show respect for others
  6. volunteer
  7. cooperate with peers and adults
  8. participate constructively in discussions and other group activities
  9. follow directions

XII. Technology Skills: The student will

1. demonstrate competence with computers

a. use word processing skills
b. use a spreadsheet
c. use a draw program
d. use a photo program
e. use hyperstudio
f. use the Internet

2. demonstrate competence with other technologies

a. use a CD drive
b. use a scanner
c. use a video recorder
d. use a video editing system
d. use an audio recording system
e. use a SLR camera
f. use a digital camera

STUDENT PERFORMANCE REQUIREMENTS
Numbers Refer To APPLICATION SKILLS

ONGOING ACTIVITIES

The students will

Maintain a Daily Log including their
- responses to a daily question
- a list of their day's activities and accomplishments
- a statement of appreciations
- an assessment of the day's quotation

[II.1, II.4, V.1, V.2, IX.1, IX.2, X.2, X.4, XI.1, XI.3, XI.9]

Complete Weekly Self-Assessment Sheets including
- assessment of week's performance in a variety of areas
- description of week's accomplishments and activities
- a goal for the coming week
- an evaluation of the previous week's goal

[II.1, II.4, V.1, IX.1, X.1, X.4, XI.1, XI.3, XI.9]

Design the Daily and Weekly Sheets
[II.4, III.2, IX.1, IX.2, IX.4, X.1, XI.7, XI.8]

Design a Class Bill of Rights
[III.2, VIII.?, IX.1, IX.2, IX.4, X.1, XI.5, XI.6, XI.7, XI.8]

Maintain a Portfolio of Work in Progress
[X.3, X.4, XI.1, XI.3, XI.9]

Plan and Conduct a Student-Led Parent Conference
[III.1, IV.1, V.1, IX.1, IX.2, IX.4, X.1, X.2, X.3, X.4, XI.1, XI.3, XI.4, XI.5, XI.9]

Plan and Produce an Evening Open House
[III.2, IV.1, IX.1, IX.2, IX.4, X.1, X.2, XI.1, XI.3, XI.4, XI.5, XI.6, XI.7, XI.8, XI.9, XII.1, XII.2]

Produce a Newsletter
[II.1, II.4, II.5, II.7, III.2, IX.1, IX.2, IX.4, X.1, X.2, XI.3, XI.4, XI.6, XI.7, XI.8, XI.9, XII.1, XII.2]

Read at Least Twenty-five (25) Books   [I.1, I.2, I.3]

Maintain a Reading Journal for each of the 25 required reading books, including the following information for various entries:
- bibliographic data in proper form
- pre-reading expectations, questions, prediction, or justification for selection

- a brief summary of the setting, plot and characters
- a representative quotation from the book and an explanation of its significance
- an explanation of literary devices used by the author
- an assessment of the book
  [I.1, I.2, II.2, II.4, II.5, V.2, VI.1, IX.1, IX.4, X.3, X.4, XI.3, XI.9]

Present at Least Three Book Talks   [I.1, I.2, IV.1, VI.1, IX.1, XI.3, XI.9]

Assess Book Talks Given by Others   [III.3, V.2, IX.1, XI.5, XI.9]

Write Formal Book Reports based on reading Journal
  [I.1, I.2, II.2, II.4, II.5, VI.1, IX.1, IX.4, X.4, XI.9, XII.1]

THEME ACTIVITIES
The students will

Brainstorm Individual Questions
1. Individually list questions
2. Small group discussion: compare, contrast, and merge individual questions
3. Share with entire class: compare, contrast, and merge individual questions
   [III.2, III.3, IV.1, V.1, V.2, VIII.?, IX.1, IX.2, IX.3, IX.4, X.1, XI.1, XI.5, XI.6, XI.7, XI.8, XI.9]

Connect Questions to Build Theme

1. Small group discussions: grouping question types, suggesting themes
2. Class discussion: grouping question types, suggesting themes
   [III.2, III.3, IV.1, V.1, V.2, VIII.?, IX.1, IX.2, IX.3, IX.4, X.1, XI.1, XI.5, XI.6, XI.7, XI.8, XI.9]

Determine Theme Through Consensus Discussion
   [III.2, III.3, IV.1, V.1, V.2, VIII.?, IX.1, IX.2, IX.3, IX.4, X.1, XI.1, XI.5, XI.6, XI.7, XI.8, XI.9]

Determine the Components of the Theme: Which questions do we want to address? What are the historical, literary, scientific, technological, societal, physical, geographical, aesthetic, cultural, and mathematic aspects of the theme?

1. Individual Brainstorming
2. Small Group Discussions
3. Class Discussion to reach consensus
   [III.2, III.3, IV.1, V.1, V.2, VIII.?, IX.1, IX.2, IX.3, IX.4, X.1, XI.1, XI.5, XI.6, XI.7, XI.8, XI.9]

<u>Determine Methods</u>: How will we explore this theme?

1. Breaking down the tasks involved: What skills will we need to develop? What information will we need to find?
2. Organizing the tasks and priorities
3. Determining possible resources
4. Planning timetables, schedules
5. Assigning responsibilities
6. Determining rubrics: How will we know we have succeeded? Benchmarks/check points along the way?
7. Determining end products: How will we show what we have learned?
   [II.4, III.2, III.3, IV.1, V.1, V.2, VIII.?, IX.1, IX.2, IX.3, IX.4, X.1, X.2, X.4, XI.1, XI.4, XI.5, XI.6, XI.7, XI.8, XI.9]

<u>Implement the Plan: Explore the Theme</u>:
   [I.1, I.2, I.3, I.4, II.1, II.4, II.5, II.6, III.1, III.2, III.3, VI.1, VII.1, VII.2, VII.3, VIII.?, IX.1, IX.2, IX.3, IX.4, X.1, X.2, X.3, X.4, XI.1, XI.2, XI.3, XI.4, XI.5, XI.6, XI.7, XI.8, XI.9, XII.1, XII.2]

<u>Create the End Product:</u> sharing our learning and accomplishments
   [II.1, II.4, II.5, II.7, III.3, IV.1, VI.2, VII.2, VII.3, VIII.?, IX.1, IX.2, IX.3, IX.4, XI.1, XI.2, XI.3, XI.4, XI.5, XI.7, XI.8, XI.9, XII.1, XII.2]

<u>Assess His or Her Work Throughout the Process</u>
   [II.1, II.4, II.5, III.1, III.2, III.3, V.1, V.2, IX.1, IX.3, X.4, XI.1, XI.3, XI.5, XI.6, XI.7, XI.8, XI.9, XII.1, XII.2]

The following chart shows how the technology unit fulfilled Pennsylvania State Standards, as they are currently benchmarked for eighth, or in some cases, ninth grade. The chart identifies the content area standards addressed by the different activities in the unit. (A schematic on p. 107 llustrates how these activities were interrelated.) A basic list of the State Standards keyed to the chart follows on pp. 211-212 . The complete and detailed list of standards can be found at the Pennsylvania Department of Education's Web site.

SOUNDINGS I: TECHNOLOGY UNIT ADDRESSING THE STATE STANDARDS

Standards / Activities	1 Language Arts	3 Science	5 Civics and Government	6 Economics	7 Geography	8 History	9 Arts and Humanities
Research Paper and Mini-Project	1.1 A,B,D,F,G 1.2 A, B 1.4 B 1.5 A, B,C, D, E, F, G 1.6 A, B, C, D,E, F 1.8 A, B,C	3.2 A 3.7 B, C, D, E Individual	Research	Topics Hit	Different	8.1 B, D Content	Standards
Fahrenheit 451	1.1 E, G, H 1.3 A, B, C, D,E, F 1.6 A, B, D, E 1.7 A, B, C	3.8 C	5.2 A, B 5.3 J, K				
12 Angry Men	1.1 E, G, H 1.3 A, B, C, D,E, F 1.6 A, B, D,E 1.7 A, B, C		5.2 A, B				
Connections Videos	1.6 A, B, D, E	3.1 C, E 3.8 A, B, C		6.2 F 6.3 B, F	7.4 A, B	8.1 A, C, D 8.4 A, C, D	9.2 A, B, C, F, G 9.4 D
Explorers and Colonial Development	1.1 A, B, C,H 1.2 A 1.4 B 1.5 A, B, C, D, E, F 1.6 A, B, D,E 1.8 A, B,C		5.1 A, B, C, D, E, 5.2 A 5.3 A, B, C, G, I, J	6.1 A, B, D 6.2 A, B, E, F 6.3 B, C 6.4 B, C, D, G 6.5 C	7.1 A, B 7.2 A 7.3 A, B, C, D,E 7.4 A, B	8.3 A, B, C, D 8.4 A, C, D	
Time Line Murals	1.6 A, B, D,E 1.8 A, B,	3.1 C, D				8.1 A, B, D	9.1 A, B, E, H 9.2 A, B, C, F,G
Trial of Galileo	1.1 A 1.2 A, C 1.4 A, B, C 1.5 A, B, C, E 1.6 A, B, D, E	3.2 A 3.8 A, B, C	5.1 J 5.2 A 5.3 J			8.1 A, B, C, D	
Experiments By Centuries	1.6 A, B, D,E 1.8 A, B	3.1 C 3.2 A, B, C 3.7 A, B 3.8 A, B, C				8.1 A, B	
Logbook	1.1 A 1.4 D 1.6 A,B, D,E 1.7 A, B, C 1.8 A, B	Log Questions	Hit Many	Areas and	Concepts	Across	Disciplines
Reading Journal	1.1 A, G,H 1.3 A, B, C, D,E, F						

PENNSYLVANIA STATE STANDARDS
for SUBJECT AREAS COVERED by INTEGRATED PROGRAMS

1. Academic Standards for Reading, Writing, Speaking and Listening
(Benchmarked grade 8)

1.1. Learning to Read Independently
1.2. Reading Critically in All Content Areas
1.3. Reading, Analyzing and Interpreting Literature
1.4. Types of Writing
1.5. Quality of Writing.
1.6. Speaking and Listening
1.7. Characteristics and Functions of the English Language
1.8. Research

3. Academic Standards for Science and Technology
(Benchmarked Grades 7 and 10)

3.1. Unifying Themes
3.2. Inquiry and Design
3.3. Biological Sciences
3.4. Physical Science, Chemistry and Physics
3.5. Earth Sciences
3.6. Technology Education
3.7. Technological Devices
3.8. Science, Technology and Human Endeavors

5. Academic Standards for Civics and Government
(Benchmarked grade 9)

5.1. Principles and Documents of Government
5.2. Rights and Responsibilities of Citizenship
5.3. How Government Works
5.4. How International Relationships Function

6. Academic Standards for Economics
(Benchmarked grade 9)

6.1. Economic Systems
6.2. Markets and the Functions of Governments
6.3. Scarcity and Choice
6.4. Economic Interdependence
6.5 . Work and Earnings

7. Academic Standards for Geography
(Benchmarked at grades 6 and 9)

7.1. Basic Geographic Literacy

7.2. The Physical Characteristics of Places and Regions

7.3. The Human Characteristics of Places and Regions

7.4. The Interactions Between People and Places

8. Academic Standards for History
(Benchmarked Grades 6 and 9)

Grades 7-9	Pennsylvania and United States 1787 to 1914	World History Beginnings to 1500

8.1. Historical Analysis and Skills Development

[Historical Analysis and Skill Development are learned through and applied to the standards statements and their descriptors for 8.2. Pennsylvania History, 8.3. United States History and 8.4. World History.]

8.2. Pennsylvania History

8.3. United States History

8.4. World History

9. Academic Standards for the Arts and Humanities
(Benchmarked Grade 8)

9.1. Production, Performance and Exhibition of Dance, Music, Theatre, and Visual Arts

9.2. Historical and Cultural Contexts

9.3. Critical Response

9.4. Aesthetic Response

APPENDIX 6

Themes from Soundings II Through Soundings VII

SOUNDINGS II: 1999–2000

For the 1999–2000 school year, students decided to create a curriculum they titled "AnthroTech." Included within this were two larger units of study. The first unit explored the creation and development of cultures. We looked first at the earth's major biomes; and the students completed group presentations such as plays and videos to explain the climate, geography, plants, and animals that create the complex ecological system in each biome. Then, students examined how these ecological conditions influenced the human cultures that developed in each biome. The students reported on existing cultures and also created hypothetical cultures to match each area. They also researched specific questions within their own personal areas of interest, wrote a research paper, and created a HyperStudio presentation to share with others.

The second unit, called simply "Technology," focused on major issues confronting our contemporary society, particularly with respect to the way society has been shaped by technology. We began by looking at major events that shaped technological progress over the last millennium. Students created a three-dimensional hanging time line of these events and described each. Then the students again selected topics of particular interest to themselves and began researching these topics for their second major research paper.

From the topics, students were placed into related groups, and the class began to create a hypothetical city to illustrate the impact of technology on many aspects of our culture. Groups looked at 11 topics ranging from the fine arts to sports and leisure, from media communications to health care, and from transportation to education. Each group then designed a representative building for our city. From their designs the students built and painted 11 "buildings" in our Activities Center transforming the 80' by 50' space into four city "blocks." Using over 75 4' by 8' panels, most of which the students had to construct, the city of New Glockamora became a thriving metropolis visited by many students from other grades, as well as parents and other guests. Inside each building, the students displayed results of their research projects and particular inventions pertaining to their group's topic area.

Students then wrote a second major research term paper about the impact of technology on an area of personal interest to them. We had papers on media influence, for example, on fuel cells, on art, on architecture, on communications, on HIV/AIDS, and on the environment, to name a few. Each student also had to use the same research topic to prepare a hanging time line entry and a PowerPoint presentation on the computer. We ended the year with group summary presentations and self-assessments.

SOUNDINGS III: 2001–2002

Why is there so much violence in our culture and our world?

In light of the tragic events on September 11, 2001, we were not at all surprised when the students decided that they wanted and needed to explore the issues of violence in our culture. Based on the questions they had devised, the class listed six areas it wanted to investigate: violence in schools, violence in the media and entertainment, violence in history, crime, terrorism, and the causes of violence. These became six working groups, each of which did significant research in preparation for a school-wide Violence Awareness Day, which we held in December.

As part of their investigation, students first learned about definitions of culture and how cultures are related to value systems. As a class, we read *The Giver* and discussed how the culture in Lowry's novel dealt with violence. We also provided supplementary readings from a variety of sources, including, for example, excerpts from the writings of Sigmund Freud and Daniel Quinn. Each student prepared a research paper based on a self-selected aspect of violence represented by the subgroup he or she had elected to join. In addition, the class held a series of debates on violence-related issues chosen by the students. Every student participated in the debates, which required additional research.

For Violence Awareness Day each group prepared some sort of presentation on its subgroup topic. The entire school was invited during the day, and the Soundings students gave six sets of performances. Then they repeated their performances in the evening for parents and other interested adults. Presentations ranged from live skits to PowerPoint programs, and every group had designed and constructed a fitting display area to augment its presentation. Central to the program was a 12-foot tall figure that the class built to represent humanity. Every person who visited our Violence Awareness Day program was asked to write down at least one compliment and at least one negative comment he or she had received. The positive comments were then pasted to the front of the statue. The negative ones were put through a shredder, and the strips were pasted on the back symbolizing that we can walk away from negativity and approach a kinder, less violent lifestyle. The day and evening were tremendous successes, and the statue went on display in our township building's lobby for Martin Luther King, Jr. Day.

How has medicine had an impact on our culture?

Our second unit of the year was quite different. The students expressed through their questions an interest in medicine and how it impacts culture. So we started by surveying the history of medicine. We created a time line of significant medical events and important people, with each student responsible for researching and presenting one entry on the time line. Then, in small groups, they examined what medical practice was like at various points in history. One group learned about ancient Greek medicine, another about ancient Chinese practices, another about Roman medicine, still another about medicine during the Renaissance, another about practices during our American Colonial period, another about medicine in 1900, and a final group looked at the mid-20th century. Each group then presented a play to demonstrate what a visit to the "doctor" of its place or time would have been like. Following the plays, each student wrote a short story on the same topic, but describing an era other than the one he or she had researched for the play.

In addition, as a class, we did a lot of supplementary reading on alternative treatments and folk remedies. Each student researched a different herbal folk remedy. Then we put together a *Soundings Compendium of Folk Remedies*, complete with drawings of the plants involved and descriptions of how the remedy was used.

We followed this with a look at modern medicine, particularly as it is played out on a cellular level. The students studied different types of human body cells, their structures, and functions. Then we looked at bacteria and viruses and how they operate within cells. Finally, we played a game of "Pathogen Pursuit" which was developed by a small committee of students working with the teachers. In this game, the class was presented with a hypothetical patient exhibiting a certain set of symptoms. Working in groups, the students had to submit questions that they thought would help them focus in on the pathogen causing the problems. Good questions yielded new information. Poor questions gave less or even erroneous information. After each round of submissions, groups could forward an answer or ask new questions. The game continued for almost a week before one group could finally name and justify the correct pathogen.

The class also tackled a second set of debates, this time on medical issues. They also worked in smaller groups to research a disease of their choice. Their presentation, however, had to focus on the research being done to combat the disease, rather than on the disease, itself. Ultimately, each group presented information to the class as if it were coming before a congressional hearing asking for funding to continue research.

Throughout this medical issues unit we had a number of guest speakers. These included a parent who is a Christian Scientist, another parent who is both a physical therapist and a practitioner of several forms of Asian alternative treatments, and a biochemist researcher from a major pharmaceutical company. These guests provided a wide range of ideas and points of view for the students to consider. We also visited several medical museums in Philadelphia to supplement the students' research for all these projects.

What would it take to live in alien environments?

Our third unit gave students the opportunity to address a number of their questions concerning the environment, culture, and new frontiers—all at the same time. "Living in Alien Environments" explored questions of the ways we interact with an environment and how some of the ways may be unique to particular places, while other interactions are common across all environments. Groups were challenged to create a sustainable society in an environment to which they were not accustomed. One group chose to "live" on Mars, for example, while another built a city underground. Three different groups tried to survive on tropical islands, while two other groups explored living beneath the oceans. Two groups elected to live in this region, but without any modern technology; and a final group explored what it would be like to try to survive in a "third-world" country that actually exists.

The groups had to prepare lengthy overviews detailing the physical, atmospheric, and biological aspects of their chosen environments. Then they designed their society and ultimately presented it to the class in the form of skits, models, and even a day in the woods. Once again, to prepare for these, the students had to write a research paper on some self-chosen aspect of their selected environment.

As a class, we read a Sonia Leviton novel entitled *The Cure*. Like *The Giver*, this novel involved a future world or culture that could not tolerate deviance. To "cure" such deviance, the elders sent a character back in time to experience anti-Semitism in Europe during the Black Plague years. This was an outstanding book, which actually tied together all three of our units.

Can we explain unexplained phenomena?

Our final unit of the year, only about two weeks in length, was a more lighthearted look at strange phenomena about which the students had initially raised questions. Ghosts, monsters, UFOs, the Bermuda Triangle, ESP, hypnotism, and other unexplained occurrences became the subjects of student-developed Web Quests and PowerPoint presentations in the closing days of school.

SOUNDINGS IV: 2002–2003

What does it mean to be human?

Our first unit this year focused on the many questions students had about themselves and what makes them who they are. In particular, the students wanted to explore how the human mind works and what the human genome is.

As part of their investigation, the students first learned about the nervous system. They studied the parts of nerve cells and the brain, the processes involved in impulse transfer through nerve cells, and how different sensory receptor cells function. Once this physiological background was established, the students explored issues related to the mind itself. They studied perceptions, memory, learning theories, imagination, and creativity. They designed experiments to test some of these concepts or their current explanations. As a class, we read *The Giver* and discussed how the culture in Lowery's novel had altered citizens' perceptions and memories. We also examined and discussed supplementary readings from a variety of sources including, for example, excerpts from the writings of Sigmund Freud and Daniel Quinn. Each student wrote several papers exploring what he or she thought all this information told us about being human.

Then we turned our attention to genetics. The students learned about the genetic materials and processes in cells. We discussed the processes through which characteristics transfer over generations and how this process is helping find causes and cures for some of the diseases that continue to plague humanity.

Throughout the unit, students researched areas of particular interest to them as individuals. Each then presented his or her findings to the class in the form of a short research paper, an oral presentation, or a PowerPoint production. In addition, the students formed groups based on common interest areas and prepared activities and presentations for their "Human Extravaganza: A View of You," to which they invited the entire school as well as their parents. Presentations ranged from live skits to PowerPoint programs, and every group had designed and constructed a fitting display area to augment its presentation.

Why can't cultures and nations seem to get along?

Our second unit of the year was quite different, but clearly related to the first. Through their questions, the students had expressed an interest in how cultures develop and then interact with each other. So we started by researching definitions of culture and how cultures are related to value systems. We read the novel, *The Last Book in the Universe,* by Rodman Philbrick. Set in the future, the novel depicts a world of genetically altered humans living well in an artificially maintained region called Eden that is surrounded by a savage and ruined world inhabited by "normal" humans now reduced to subsistence or barbarian existence. As the young protagonist quests through this world, he learns a great deal about how fear, love, greed, and need affect the ways humans treat each other on both individual and societal levels. The students then formed into four randomly selected groups, each of which was given a portion of a realistic, yet hypothetical continent. Each group had to create a culture that would realistically develop in an environment such as the one represented in its own part of the continent. They developed this culture's religion, government, economy, and all other aspects common to human cultures, describing the culture's progress from its creation myth to an early industrialized state similar to our world around 1800. In addition, the students each did a research paper on some aspect of culture as it exists in reality and how that aspect would be applied to that made-up culture.

Then, we played a game of cultural interaction. In this game, each day represented a new decade or so. Groups drew from cards detailing changes in the natural environment (floods, earthquakes, forest fires, etc.), the economic environment, the political environment, and technological advancements or discoveries. Each culture then had to respond to all these changes. The nature of the changes forced the cultures into contact with one another, much as nations and cultures really are. Alliances and trading groups formed, hypothetical wars were waged, sub-sects broke off and declared independence. In short, a very realistic world developed among these pretend nations. Along the way, students wrote three papers to illustrate how their culture changed over the course of the game. One paper was a series of letters or diary entries from characters living in the culture. A second was a short story describing how the culture reacted to one of the major events that occurred, and the last was a newspaper editorial presenting opinions on some change within the culture.

We then threw into the mix questions of resource depletion, and we began to explore the concept of sustainability. The class wrote an Earth Charter outlining the aspects of cultures that ought to be sustained and suggested ways to accomplish that sustainability. Then we read the UN Earth Charter and compared it to our own.

The class also tackled a set of debates on real conflict issues. Small groups researched real-world conflicts, such as Iraq, Northern Ireland, the Koreas, the Ivory Coast, and Palestine. Then they subdivided to represent the two major sides of each conflict and, after further research and preparation, debated their causes in front of the class.

What is time, and how is it related to the universe?

Our third and final unit gave the students the opportunity to address a number of their questions concerning the physical universe and our perceptions of time. Again, though at first this appears quite different from the previous two units, the students quickly saw major areas of overlap with respect to human perceptions and the need to understand and order our existence.

Small groups again selected mini-topics such as the solar system, gravity, black holes, stars, and so forth. They researched their area and then taught the rest of us about how that topic helped us understand the way time and our universe are interconnected. We read the opening chapter on Stephen Hawking's *A Brief History of Time,* as well as smaller articles on the history of telling time.

The students challenged themselves to develop unusual ways to time a minute. Some truly creative and remarkable inventions began to appear in the room, and we had fun testing each to see how accurate it was. The students then pushed themselves even further to try and build mechanical clocks that could actually tell time, not just measure one minute. Again a great deal of thinking, research, and creativity went into the resulting contraptions.

Simultaneously, we began to look at relativity, theories of the expanding universe, and the concept of alternate universes as currently being researched by a number of astrophysicists. As a class, we read a Sonia Leviton novel entitled *The Cure*. Like *The Giver*, this novel involved a future world or culture that could not tolerate deviance. To "cure" such deviance, the elders sent a character back in time to experience anti-Semitism in Europe during the Black Plague years. This was an outstanding book that actually tied together all three of our units. We also read Ray Bradbury's short story, "A Sound of Thunder" about the consequences of time travel, and the students wrote their own stories of time travel or of visiting an alternate universe.

SOUNDINGS V: 2003–2004
(This description written by Mary Canniff)

Dreams

Our first unit of the year focused on physical dreams, specifically what happens to the human body during dreams and if dreams have meaning.

To answer what happens physically, we began by studying the brain. We looked at what roles individual chemicals play during the cycles of sleep and during dreaming. Along with the physical chemistry of dreams, we examined how dreams have played a historic role. We read a selection from Aristotle's "On Dreams," and accompanied it with poems selected by Stephen Brock. The students used their individual research skills to answer a variety of issues, and each student wrote a paper discussing whether or not his or her research supported the idea that dreams can be interpreted. As a class we read Lois Lowry's *Gathering Blue*, discussing the importance of dreaming to the central character, Kira. Students also wrote a paper examining the themes present in the novel.

The students elected to present their findings to the rest of the student body of Radnor Middle School with a Dream Fair. The idea was that the visiting groups would be in a dream as they entered the activity center and visited 5 of the 15 booths the Soundings students had created. These booths included games, skits, PowerPoint presentations, dances, and even a dream interpretation booth. Students had first presented their information informally to the class, revised it for their Dream Fair presentations, and produced it in written form. Those essays were student edited into a Dream Book. We also had an evening presentation so that the students' family could come see their work.

Culture

In order to answer the many questions they had about culture, the students divided into eight groups of five based on specific aspects of culture: belief systems, governments, economics, language/communication/transportation, food, clothing, recreation and arts, and family structure. Concurrently, the class divided into five continent groups consisting of one student from each aspect group.

As a class, we read several articles and excerpts dealing with culture, including "The Lottery" by Shirley Jackson and selections from *Ishmael* by Daniel Quinn. We also read our second novel of the year, *The Cure*, written by Sonia Levinson. Through discussion we examined what these readings showed us about how culture is developed and defined. As we read these selections, the aspect groups presented their findings on culture to the rest of the class. Each group typically took a week to cover its information, using techniques such as handouts, simulations, outlines, group activities, and guest speakers. The students wrote several papers including a persuasive paper on the best type of government and a narrative alternative ending to *The Cure*. The students also completed their first research project of the year. The students self-selected a topic related to culture and completed a structured process to complete their papers.

To assess the culture unit as a whole, the students elected to make "mocumentaries" in the style of reality television shows, specifically "The Amazing Race." Each continent group was responsible for making an episode of the reality show based on the cultures of its continent. The continent groups all wrote scripts that illustrated examples of all eight aspects of cultures from at least five cultures indigenous to their continent. The project also involved creating storyboards and scenery, filming, and digitally editing the video.

Animals

To finish our year, the students were evenly split between two umbrella questions. Therefore, we had half of our students investigating theories and reasons behind evolution, and the other half examined how humans affect animals.

We started off with introductions to theories of evolution and to basic genetics. We used readings from a variety of sources, including several textbooks and magazines. An additional source consisted of several short videos illustrating several pertinent concepts such as cell evolution, animal adaptation, environmental causes of evolution, homologous forms, and human impact on animals. Students formed groups based on what questions they wanted answered. The evolution group addressed such topics as mass extinction, the chronology of evolution, and what possible future evolutions might be. The group studying how humans affect animals examined issues such as animal abuse, animal testing, domestication, and endangered animals. After a month of research, each student group presented its findings to the class as a whole.

A second research paper was also assigned during this unit. Students self-managed the due dates of each step of the project. Again, the students could choose any topic of interest as long as the subject related to animals. Many chose to write a topic related to their particular group, but many also branched off into topics not addressed otherwise by the class.

As the culminating project for the animal unit, the students divided into two groups based on interest. One group chose to raise money for the World Wildlife Federation by making and selling bracelets, anklets, and necklaces. The other group chose to produce a Web page. Each student agreed to provide an article, based on his or her research, for the Web group to publish.

SOUNDINGS VI: 2004–2005

Human body

Our first unit of the year focused on the functions and dysfunctions of the human body. The unit began with a review of the systems of the human body. The class divided into ten groups and made two-minute informative music videos to describe the circulatory system, the respiratory system, the nervous system, the skeletal system, the muscular system, the excretory system, the endocrine system, and the digestive system, as well as evolutionary theory and different medical practices. Students also wrote a reflective essay on the experience of writing and shooting the video.

Concurrently, the students also chose to be part of a specific disease or dysfunction group such as yellow fever, Down's syndrome, depression, or eating disorders. Each group produced a summary page for the class, presented its findings to the class, and created a poster to display in the hall to share the information with the rest of the school.

As a class we also read *The Cure* by Sonia Levitin and examined it for viewpoints on disease and societal views on being different. The students also wrote a narrative alternative ending to the novel. While we read and discussed the novel, the students chose groups to learn about the different parts and functions of the brain. They decided to present the information to the seventh grade, and the sixth-grade integrative program, Crossroads, through rotating presentations in the lower gym. As guests arrived, they passed by a large painted ear, a drawing of the inner ear connection to the brain, and then through a seven-foot tall, student-constructed "Big Brain." The guests then proceeded to "stations" where they completed activities designed and run by Soundings students to educate them about the cerebellum, the cerebrum, the frontal lobe, the medulla oblongata, the occipital lobe, the parietal lobe, the pituitary gland and corpus callosum, and the temporal lobe.

To conclude our human body unit, the students completed a Limitations Olympics. Each group designed an experiment to test a dimension of human capacity such as strength, speed, flexibility, balance, or memory. Each group then conducted the experiment on all Soundings students, gathered data, and wrote a lab report presenting its findings.

Culture and arts

The second unit involved us in an exploration of several different cultures. The students selected Ancient Egypt (Second Kingdom), first century Rome, tenth century Viking, 12th century England, 13th century France, 15th century Japan, and contemporary China. For each of these cultures, groups of students researched the foods, clothing, sports, arts, and language. Then the groups devised different ways to share their research so we could compare and contrast the cultures. They each held a feast day, for example, that included a detailed menu and description of the importance of food in that culture. Representative foods were then served in the manner of the times. On another day, the class held a runway fashion show of the clothing worn in the culture it studied; and on another day it had an art museum of representative artworks. We spent several days playing sports and board or card games from the cultures, and two days examining their languages.

The unit culminated in a museum of the seven cultures with displays of all the materials used in the various days described. The centerpiece for each culture was a scale model town constructed on a four-foot by four-foot base. Students created suitable topography and background scenery. They researched the types of buildings and the styles of architecture, and they built models of the buildings to create a hypothetical town. This museum was opened to the parents one evening, and to the rest of the school over two days. The students acted as docents guiding tours of the cultural museum.

In addition to all this group work, each student was responsible for the first of two research papers on a topic of his or her own choosing. This project, broken into segments such as outlines and rough drafts, spanned the two months of the unit. Students also read a second novel that related to cultures. This time, however, the class used the technique of literature circles, with different circles reading one of four different novels. We used *The Hobbit; Gathering Blue; The Ear, the Eye and the Arm;* and *The Wizard of Earthsea.*

Exploring above and below: Space and the oceans

For this third and final unit of the year, the students elected to explore the unknown, literally. They wanted to see how mankind's exploration of oceans compares to our explorations of outer space. They were particularly interested in myths and legends about oceans and space, and also about life in the oceans. The steering committee, with the advice and consent of the class, decided to pursue several different projects. Two large murals were planned and designed: one of life in the ocean at various depths and one of objects in space. Each student researched an animal and a space object for the murals, and together created a booklet for each mural describing the animals and objects depicted. In addition, the students built a walk-in model of the submersible, *Alvin,* and one of the cockpit of a space shuttle from which to view the murals as if one were actually under the sea or in space.

In addition to this major undertaking—which by the way turned out to be extraordinary—the students also studied elements of oceanography, such as bathymetrics, plate tectonics, currents, waves, salinity, and density. They looked at how different pelagic zones affect the organisms that live in each. They also made a time line to illustrate the history of undersea exploration from ancient Greek sponge divers to the present day.

A similar examination of space exploration included adding its historical events to the time line of ocean exploration to compare the two. We discussed the various major space programs including Sputnik, followed by Mercury, Gemini, Apollo, and the unmanned satellite ventures such as Voyager I and II. Students also studied some basic physics of acceleration and gravity; and then they learned about the work of Copernicus, Kepler, Gallileo, Newton, and Einstein. They discussed the Big Bang and various theories concerning the state and the future of the universe.

Paralleling these studies, the students wrote several essays and participated in a series of formal debates on topics related to oceans and space. They also planned and wrote their second major research paper of the year. Again, each student selected a topic of personal interest, the only stipulation being that it have something to do with either oceans or space. Topics ranged from oceanic myths of the Maori to how ocean currents affect weather, and from the role of constellation mythology to the physics of black holes.

SOUNDINGS VII: 2005–2006

What are some cutting edge technologies affecting our life?

For this first unit, the students decided to study two topics as a class —genetics and nanotechnology. Using these as examples, they would apply what they were learning to smaller group projects covering a wide variety of areas in which the students had interest. Our work on genetics took us through a review of the history from Mendel through Watson and Crick to today's researchers. We learned about the RNA and DNA processes at the cellular level, and we learned to use punnet squares to determine odds of dominant and recessive characteristics. On one field trip to the Maryland Science Center in Baltimore, many students learned to extract DNA from wheat, while all were able to learn more about genetics at the exhibits there.

As a class, we also watched and discussed a video on the Genographic Project that has been attempting to trace the spread of the human genome around the globe. A parent of one of our students has participated in the project, and she shared her results with us. We followed up on all this with formal debates about cloning and about genetic medical research of various sorts, before turning our attention to nanotechnology.

This short but interesting section of the unit quickly revealed that what the students had thought about nanotechnology was not, in truth, what it is. They envisioned it with respect simply to making items smaller, as in the so-called "nano" iPods and MP3 players they now enjoy using. Our research as a class revealed a much more sophisticated and complex world of experimentation in scales as unimaginably small as a millionth of a millimeter. We read a number of articles on this truly cutting-edge science and its many future implications.

We read *The Last Book in the Universe* together as a class. It is a science fiction novel set in a future post-catastrophe world in which genetic engineering has divided the remaining population into different societies. The novel allowed us to look at many of the same issues we were seeing in our research work, but from a different perspective. It also served as a great transition into our second unit, but more on that momentarily.

As mentioned at the onset, the students designed this unit so they could work in small groups on specific areas in which cutting-edge technologies are having an impact. Each student served on two committees investigating topics such as computers, robotics, music technology, medical technology, transportation technology, communications, and even household appliances. Each group presented its findings to the class using models, posters, and demonstrations.

Each student also tackled his or her first of two individual research paper projects. Here again they could select any area they wanted. The only condition required them to relate it to technology somehow. Of course, this presented no problem, and we received papers on a wide range of interesting topics.

We culminated the unit with a second field trip, this time to the Franklin Institute. There students had the chance to visit the Body Worlds exhibit, which related to all our work in genetics. They also had opportunities to visit the permanent exhibits, such as the one on the human body and others specifically describing cutting-edge contemporary technologies in many different fields.

How do businesses function?

For our second unit this year, the students elected to look in-depth at economics and business. This was truly a first in Soundings. As a class we learned about basic economic concepts and theories. We looked at the history of economics, in particular at how the United States began and developed due to a number of important economic issues such as mercantilism, colonialism, and laissez-faire policies. We compared and contrasted economic theories of capitalism, socialism, and communism. We learned about scarcity, and supply and demand. We studied the stock market, tracked stock performances for the 12 weeks of our unit, and graphed our results.

The novel we read at the close of our technology unit, *The Last Book in the Universe*, intentionally overlapped into the onset of the economics unit. A great deal of the plot concerned legal and illegal commerce among the peoples of the future world, and different sectors of that world were organized along principles of different economic systems. Hence the novel formed an excellent bridge connecting the two units as it put the economic theories into realistic images for the students.

As in their first unit, the students wanted to devote much of their time to smaller group projects. They felt, however, that their previous attempt to complete two separate group projects had perhaps been a bit overly ambitious. This time they opted to concentrate on just one. Their format was to create a hypothetical business, write an actual business plan based on their research, and then present their concept to students and parents who would act as prospective investors, employees, or customers and assess the presentations and the businesses accordingly.

First we listed 30 or so possible types of businesses in which they might be interested. Students then individually ranked their favorites, and 13 groups formed based on those preferences. Each newly formed group then selected a specific business from its mutual area of interest. We ended up with a veterinary clinic, a hospital, a convenience food store, a cruise line company, a sporting goods retailer, a recording company, a non-profit summer camp for disadvantaged youths, a bookstore, a restaurant, two advertising agencies, a community theatre, and a plastic bag manufacturer.

After weeks of research, interviews, visits, planning, and writing, the groups presented their hypothetical businesses to their parents one evening at a Soundings Business Fair. This dress rehearsal prepared the students for two subsequent days of presenting the Business Fair to the entire seventh and eighth grades through their social studies classes. The presentations were so thorough that a large number of student visitors were convinced the businesses actually existed!

How do our beliefs affect our actions?

Our third unit for this Soundings VII year is just being planned as I write this. As the umbrella question states, it is a unit on how beliefs and actions are interrelated. We are currently looking at general definitions of belief systems, world-views, and creation myths. We have read Shirley Jackson's short story, "The Lottery," and an excerpt from Daniel Quinn's novel, *Ishmael,* both of which pose questions about the nature of beliefs and actions.

Though the final outcomes will be determined shortly, all I can say at present is that the class is leaning toward looking at major world issues and historic events as a focus toward which to turn the students' lens of belief systems. The current religious, political, and economic situation in Iraq and the rest of the Middle East has been mentioned, as has been the Holocaust, violence in schools, and the role of youth in different cultures. My guess is the class will decide to select one or two as case studies again, and then move back into smaller groups to examine more closely subtopics of particular interest. Whatever the students decide, it promises to be an exciting final unit with great opportunities for debates, for involving literature and writing, and for examining the very democratic ideals that are the foundation of the Soundings philosophy.